What other people are sayin

"Pat Williams is a great leader and a m... God's Way, will expand your leadership style and show you what it looks like to lead like Christ. Take some time to read how you can better impact your people by leading like Christ."

RICK WARREN, SENIOR PASTOR OF SADDLEBACK CHURCH, LAKE FOREST, CA

"Leading God's Way is a fascinating journey through the lives of some of the great leaders of the Bible. Pat Williams has a gift for applying the timeless truths of God's Word to our leadership lives today. The discussion guide makes this book an excellent resource for leadership teams and Bible study groups. I recommend it!"

DR. DAVID JEREMIAH, SENIOR PASTOR OF SHADOW MOUNTAIN
COMMUNITY CHURCH, EL CAJON, CALIFORNIA

"The Bible is filled with great leadership role models. Pat Williams—one of the top leaders in the sports world, the business world, and the Christian world—has delved deeply into the Bible and produced a treasury of leadership wisdom. Whether your leadership arena is your home, your church, or your company, Leading God's Way is the book you and your leadership team need to read."

DR. ROBERT JEFFRESS, SENIOR PASTOR OF FIRST BAPTIST CHURCH, DALLAS

"Leaders are readers and reading this book is a must! It gives you information and inspiration passed along in the typical Pat Williams style. He knows how to lead and he knows his Bible; this book is a powerful combination of both. If you take Pat's words seriously, reading these pages will not only hold your attention but it will change your life. He takes leadership seriously and so should you. This book is great!"

DR. WARREN WIERSBE, AUTHOR AND RADIO MINISTER

"Leadership is complicated and challenging. Yet Pat Williams has done a marvelous job of digesting leadership into its most basic, easy-to-understand principles. From the eight biblical characters used as examples, to the seven immutable sides of leadership, Pat has revealed to leaders everywhere how to make leadership work and how they can become successful in God's eyes. Thanks, Pat! Another great book from a very successful leader."

DAVID CHADWICK, SENIOR PASTOR OF FOREST HILL CHURCH, CHARLOTTE

"Pat Williams has outdone himself with this inspirational and practical book on biblical leadership! You can't read this without ushering deeper and more effective leadership in your life."

DR. JOEL C. HUNTER, FAITH COMMUNITY ORGANIZER; MANAGING CHAIR, COMMUNITY RESOURCE NETWORK;
MANAGING CHAIR, CENTRAL FLORIDA COMMISSION ON HOMELESSNESS

"Pat Williams has written another valuable book. Biblical leaders have much to teach us about vision, communication, and other leadership skills. Get ready for an invaluable read. And be sure to have a pen or marker with you … you will be using it a lot!"

FRED LUTER, SENIOR PASTOR OF FRANKLIN AVENUE BAPTIST CHURCH, NEW ORLEANS; FORMER PRESIDENT OF THE SOUTHERN BAPTIST CONVENTION

"My friend Pat Williams has always been an incredible example of leveraging His job, skill and passion for the glory of God. In his new book, Leading God's Way, *he once again uses his years of leadership experience to point people to the ultimate source of wisdom and truth: the Word of God. This book will challenge you as a leader and inspire you to deepen your faith as you explore the unfathomable riches of God's word. Thanks, Pat, for another investment in leaders everywhere!"*

VANCE H. PITMAN, SENIOR PASTOR OF HOPE CHURCH, LAS VEGAS

Pat Williams knows how to lead. He's done it in world-class fashion with the Orlando Magic. He also knows how to teach leadership, which is something else entirely. I was drawn into his narrative immediately as he wove together the stories of heroes, both ancient and modern. Leading God's Way *is both direct and profound. The principles Pat uncovers in the life of Jesus and other biblical leaders are easy to understand but often hard to implement. Pat speaks powerfully to students and practitioners. Study groups will find his discussion questions both stimulating and thought-provoking. Any person who wants to lead in a godly way should read this book."*

DAVID E. CROSBY, PASTOR, FIRST BAPTIST NEW ORLEANS

"I've had the privilege to get to know Pat Williams as an unquestioned authority on leadership. His latest book confirms this. Leading God's Way *will make a difference in many lives and be a catalyst for reviving biblical leadership. I recommend this book with great enthusiasm."*

DR. GREGORY THORNBURY, PRESIDENT OF THE KING'S COLLEGE, NEW YORK CITY

"Leadership is a skill that is both caught and taught. The best way to know how to lead is by following the example of the great and godly leaders like those we meet in the Bible. My friend, Pat Williams, knows his Bible and he knows leadership. In Leading God's Way *you will discover divine principles and pathways to an authentic influence which will not only help you become a Bible leader, but also a better person. This book is leadership gold!"*

DR. JACK GRAHAM, PASTOR, PRESTONWOOD BAPTIST CHURCH, PLANO, TX

LEADING
GOD'S
WAY

LEADING GOD'S WAY

LESSONS FROM THE LIVES OF
GREAT LEADERS OF THE BIBLE

PAT WILLIAMS

WITH *JIM DENNEY*

Advantage®

Published by Advantage, Charleston, South Carolina.
Member of Advantage Media Group.

ADVANTAGE is a registered trademark, and the Advantage colophon is a trademark of Advantage Media Group, Inc.

Printed in the United States of America.

10 9 8 7 6 5 4 3 2 1

ISBN: 978-1-59932-884-3
LCCN: 2017961697

Cover design by George Stevens.
Layout design by Carly Blake.

This publication is designed to provide accurate and authoritative information in regard to the subject matter covered. It is sold with the understanding that the publisher is not engaged in rendering legal, accounting, or other professional services. If legal advice or other expert assistance is required, the services of a competent professional person should be sought.

 Advantage Media Group is proud to be a part of the Tree Neutral® program. Tree Neutral offsets the number of trees consumed in the production and printing of this book by taking proactive steps such as planting trees in direct proportion to the number of trees used to print books. To learn more about Tree Neutral, please visit **www.treeneutral.com.**

Advantage Media Group is a publisher of business, self-improvement, and professional development books. We help entrepreneurs, business leaders, and professionals share their Stories, Passion, and Knowledge to help others Learn & Grow. Do you have a manuscript or book idea that you would like us to consider for publishing? Please visit advantagefamily.com or call **1.866.775.1696.**

This book
is gratefully dedicated to
David Uth, Danny de Armas, and Jimmy Knott,
three magnificent leaders
at First Baptist Church, Orlando.

CONTENTS

ACKNOWLEDGMENTS

*I deeply appreciate the support and guidance of the people
who helped make this book possible:*

Special thanks to Alex Martins, Dan DeVos, and Rich DeVos
of the Orlando Magic.

Hats off to my associate Andrew Herdliska; my proofreader,
Ken Hussar; and my ace typist, Fran Thomas.

Thanks also to my writing partner, Jim Denney,
for his superb contributions in shaping this manuscript.

Hearty thanks also go to Adam Witty and the Advantage Media
Group team for their vision and insight, and for believing we had
something important to say in these pages.

And, finally, special thanks and appreciation go to
my wife, Ruth, and to my wonderful and supportive family.
They are truly the backbone of my life.

INTRODUCTION

In my writing and speaking, I have found that everything that needs to be said about leadership can be organized into what I call The Seven Sides of Leadership:

1. *Vision*

2. *Communication*

3. *People Skills*

4. *Good Character*

5. *Competence*

6. *Boldness*

7. *Servanthood*

All of the great leaders in the Bible had most of these seven essential ingredients, and Jesus exemplified *all seven* dimensions. Though Jesus is the ultimate example of what it means to lead God's way, there are other instructive examples of godly leadership in the Old and New Testaments. The great saints of Bible times have much to teach us twenty-first century saints about effective, world-changing leadership.

Some Bible leaders were outstanding examples of one particular dimension. For example, Joseph, in the Book of Genesis, has much to teach us about competence, boldness, and servanthood, but the one dimension that shouts to us above all others is his good character, his integrity, and his iron determination to avoid sin. And though we see great boldness, character, and people skills in the life of Queen Esther, she is, above all, an example of a leader with a serving heart.

The Bible is so rich in leadership examples that this book easily could have been a thousand or ten thousand pages long. There are many more biblical leaders I wish I could have written about in this book, but I hope this book sparks a sense of excitement within you as you study the lives of great leaders of the Bible.

And above all, I hope you discover new dimensions of what it means to lead God's way.

CHAPTER 1

JESUS: THE COMPLETE LEADER

On June 6, 1982, the Israel Defense Forces invaded southern Lebanon in response to repeated attacks by the Palestine Liberation Organization in Lebanon. By August, the rolling battles between the warring forces had left West Beirut in rubble. Word came out of Lebanon that a number of children were huddled in the abandoned and battle-scarred Dar al-Ajaza al-Islamia Hospital in West Beirut. The ongoing shelling and street battles made it impossible for rescue workers to reach the hospital.

One little Albanian nun decided to do what no one else dared. Her name was Mother Teresa, and she had spent her adult life ministering to the poor and sick in India. Now she was on a different mission. She had to enter the war zone of West Beirut and save the children.

She couldn't fly in—the airport was destroyed—but a Palestinian group offered to take her by ferry boat from Cyprus to Beirut. She agreed. Arriving in Cyprus, she learned that the "ferry boat" was a Palestinian gun-running boat. She had no choice but to go with the gun-runners. Her only companions were two Canadian filmmakers, Anne Petrie and Jeanette Petrie, who were shooting a documentary about Mother Teresa's life. As they boarded the boat, Mother Teresa said to the Petrie sisters, "I have brought a candle to Our Lady of Peace. When we get to Beirut we will light this candle, and we will have peace."

During the sea crossing to Beirut, the Petrie sisters briefly panicked when they couldn't find Mother Teresa. She'd simply disappeared. They eventually found her below decks, doing what any true servant would do—she was in the "head" (the lavatory), scrubbing the filthy toilet.

Mother Teresa and her companions were set ashore on the beach. They made their way around the southern outskirts of the city to the Spring School in East Beirut, operated by Mother Teresa's Missionaries of Charity. She met with two priests and a monsignor to discuss the rescue plan. Artillery shells screamed and exploded in the distance as they talked.

The priests recommended patience. Wait until the current military action is over. Right now, it's simply too dangerous. But Mother Teresa insisted that her place was there, with the children. Her Christian duty was not to stay safe, but to save the children.

The priests reminded Mother Teresa that terrorists had recently killed several Catholic workers just for the sake of killing. West Beirut was in chaos. Yes, it was their job to risk their lives to save others— but for the sake of the children, they needed a plan with a strong possibility of success.

Mother Teresa said, "What if both sides stop fighting for a few hours?"

The priests saw little hope of that.

"All for Jesus," Mother Teresa said. "We have to start. Many years back, I picked up the first person off the street in Calcutta. If I didn't pick up that first person, I never would have picked up 42,000 in Calcutta. So we must go."

A short time later, Mother Teresa met with Philip Habib, President Reagan's Special Envoy to the Middle East. She told him, "I need your help to cross over into West Beirut. I'm going to rescue some children."

"Mother Teresa," Mr. Habib said, "do you hear the artillery shells?"

"Yes, I hear them."

"It's impossible for you to cross. There must be a cease-fire first."

"I have been praying. I have asked for a cease-fire tomorrow."

"Mother Teresa, I believe in prayer. I am a man of faith. But don't you think the time limit is rather short?"

"Oh, no, Mr. Habib, I am certain we will have a cease-fire tomorrow."

"If the cease-fire occurs, I will personally make the arrangements to get you into West Beirut tomorrow."

The next morning, Israel and the PLO made a stunning announcement. Both sides had agreed to a cease-fire. Ambassador Habib arranged for a Red Cross convoy to take Mother Teresa to West Beirut.

Anne Petrie and Jeanette Petrie filmed the scene as Mother Teresa and the Red Cross workers entered the war-ravaged hospital. Some of the children they found were mentally disabled, some had cerebral palsy, most were suffering from starvation. They had been without care for days.

Mother Teresa hugged the children and cleaned them up. One emaciated little boy lay in a crib, his body trembling, his eyes wide with fear. He'd spent days in filth, without food, with the sound of artillery and bombs all around. Mother Teresa bent over him, rubbed his chest, stroked his hair, smiled at him, and told him, "I love you. Jesus loves you." He stopped trembling, and he no longer seemed afraid.

Mother Teresa and the Red Cross took thirty-seven children in four vehicles. They brought them to the Spring School—mission accomplished.[1]

If not for Mother Teresa's Christlike leadership, those children would have died in the rubble of that abandoned hospital. She prayed for a cease-fire, and God answered her prayer—the war clouds parted before her like the Red Sea parting before Moses.

Mother Teresa was a complete leader. She followed the example of Jesus the Master. She exemplified what I call the Seven Sides of Leadership.

She led God's way.

THE GREATEST LEADER WHO EVER LED

Many years ago, an American minister, Dr. James Allan Francis (1864–1928), wrote a short essay called "One Solitary Life," about the life of Jesus:

Here is a man who was born in an obscure village, the child of a peasant woman. He grew up in another obscure village, where He worked in a carpenter shop until He was thirty, and then for three years He was an itinerant preacher. He never wrote a book. He never held an office. He never owned a home. He never had a family. He never went to college. He never put his foot inside a big city. He never traveled two hundred miles from the place where He was born. He never did one of the things that usually accompany greatness....

Nineteen wide centuries have come and gone and today He is the centerpiece of the human race and the leader of the column of progress. I am far within the mark when I say that all the armies that ever marched, and all the navies that ever were built, and all the parliaments that ever sat, all the kings that ever reigned, put together, have not affected the life of man upon this earth as powerfully as has that One Solitary Life.[2]

When you look at Jesus in those terms, His achievement becomes truly astonishing. H. G. Wells once wrote, "I am an historian, I am not a believer, but I must confess as a historian that this penniless preacher from Nazareth is irrevocably the very center of history. Jesus Christ is easily the most dominant figure in all history." It's true. Jesus began his leadership journey by investing his life in twelve uneducated men. Today, the Christian faith numbers more than 2.5 billion people.

Any leader who can start with so little and accomplish so much across a span of so many years is a leader we should study. That's why I am opening this book with the leadership model of Jesus. Ed Stetzer, executive director of the Billy Graham Center at Wheaton College, offers this perspective on Jesus as a leadership role model:

> Jesus did not come to be your leadership guru. He came to die on the cross, for your sin, and in your place.
>
> Yet, he did lead. And we can learn from how he led. If we look closely, we see that his leadership was wrapped in humility and servanthood. Even for those in high leadership positions, we all ultimately submit to one Person, and that is the Lord Jesus Christ.[3]

Over the years, I have found that everything that needs to be said about leadership can be organized into what I call The Seven Sides of Leadership: Vision, Communication Skills, People Skills, Good Character, Competence, Boldness, and A Serving Heart. These are the seven traits every great leader must have. If you lack any one of these traits, you will be incomplete as a leader.

It shouldn't surprise us that Jesus possessed of all these traits in abundance. All the great leaders of the Bible have most of these seven essential ingredients, but Jesus exemplified all seven. He's the ultimate example of what it means to lead God's way. Let's look at how Jesus exemplified each of The Seven Sides of Leadership.

JESUS, THE VISIONARY LEADER

Jesus had a vision for a special community He called "the Kingdom of Heaven." One Sabbath day at the outset of His ministry, Jesus went to the synagogue in Nazareth, took the scroll of the Book of Isaiah, and began reading:

> The Spirit of the Lord is on me,
> because he has anointed me
> to proclaim good news to the poor.
> He has sent me to proclaim freedom for the prisoners
> and recovery of sight for the blind,
> to set the oppressed free,
> to proclaim the year of the Lord's favor.
> (Luke 4:18-19 NIV)

Jesus rolled up the scroll, gave it back to the attendant, and sat down. Then He said, "Today this Scripture is fulfilled in your hearing." The people in the synagogue were astonished because Jesus had done something that was never done—he had stopped reading in mid-sentence. Many in the congregation knew this famous passage of Old Testament Scripture by heart. Jesus had omitted the phrase, "and the day of vengeance of our God."

Why did Jesus leave out the prophecy of God's day of vengeance? He did so because God's day of vengeance would come later in history. Jesus had come to fulfill the first part of that prophecy. He had come with a mission of proclaiming the good news of freedom, healing, and God's grace toward the human race.

When Jesus said, "Today this scripture is fulfilled in your hearing," He was saying, in effect, "I am the fulfillment of this Old Testament prophecy. I am here to preach the good news to the poor. I am here to announce God's blessing to humanity." In other words, Jesus was declaring Himself to be the long-promised Messiah.

At first, the people of Nazareth were impressed by the words of Jesus. But as the full meaning of his words sank in, they asked each other, "Isn't this man the son of Joseph the carpenter? And now he claims to be the Messiah?" The people had heard that Jesus had performed miracles in nearby Capernaum, and they wanted Jesus to perform miracles for them. They also thought that if He was the Messiah, he would lead a revolt against Roman oppression.

But Jesus refused to put on a show of miracles for them, and refused to lead a revolution. So the people of Nazareth turned against him. They dragged him to the edge of a cliff, intending to throw him into the canyon below. But Jesus shrugged off their hands, walked through the middle of the crowd, and went on His way.

From then on, Jesus went around the countryside, proclaiming His vision of the Kingdom of Heaven. To carry out his vision, Jesus chose twelve men of untested ability, from unlikely backgrounds. At least four of the men—Peter, Andrew, James, and John— were fishermen and probably illiterate. One of them, Matthew, was a social outcast, a tax collector for the Roman government. Another, Simon the Zealot, was an extremist, a political troublemaker. There wasn't a single impressive resumé among them.

If you wanted to change the world, would you have chosen these twelve individuals? Yet Jesus saw potential in them and He poured His life into them. He taught them, trained them, challenged them, and mentored them. He threw them into sink-or-swim situations and He molded them into an unstoppable force for change.

Jesus invested extra time with one particular disciple, Simon Peter. He had a vision of Simon's future, and He gave Simon a new name to match that vision. Jesus told him, "You are Simon son of John. You will be called Peter" (John 1:42 NIV). The Greek name "Peter" means "Rock." Yet when Jesus called Peter, he was anything but a rock. He was unstable, impulsive, and unreliable. But Jesus had a vision of Peter as a walking Rock of Gibraltar, so He gave him a new name and a new vision of himself. In time, Peter learned to live up to that name.

Jesus never settled for what a person was. He was always more focused on what a person could become. Those who encountered Jesus were changed by his vision for their lives—and His vision for a changed world, a vision of the Kingdom of Heaven.

JESUS, THE COMMUNICATING LEADER

If a leader can't communicate the vision to others, how can that leader lead? Who will follow a leader who doesn't communicate?

Jesus communicated His vision of the Kingdom in many ways. As Malcolm Muggeridge observed, "Jesus' good news, then, was that the Kingdom of God had come, and that He, Jesus, was its herald and expounder to men. More than that, in some special and mysterious way, He *was* the kingdom."

The most significant way Jesus communicated His vision was through the message known as the Sermon on the Mount. What was the Sermon on the Mount about? Well, it's about many different things—how to be blessed, how to make a difference in the world, how to overcome temptation and sin, how to live in harmony with others, and how to seek our security in God instead of riches.

But ultimately, the Sermon on the Mount is about *one* thing: *What it means to be a citizen of the Kingdom of Heaven.* Jesus lays out how a citizen of heaven is supposed to think and act. Every thought and action Jesus speaks about in the Sermon on the Mount is a facet of the way Jesus thought and acted when He walked among us.

Jesus described himself as a king—but as he told the Roman governor Pontius Pilate, His kingdom is not of this world. The Kingdom of Heaven operates by a different set of principles than any other kingdom on earth. The principles of the Kingdom of Heaven are not like man-made laws. They are not laws that impose punishments for disobedience. They are promises that offer rewards for those who obey.

The principles of the Kingdom of Heaven are frequently paradoxical. Again and again in the Sermon, Jesus astonishes us with the principles of his Kingdom. We expect the rich and powerful to be happy and blessed. Jesus tells us that the lowly, the humble, the sorrowing, the righteous, the persecuted, and the powerless are truly blessed.

Jesus communicates his vision of the Kingdom through a series of vivid contrasts. The world is tasteless, but the citizens of His Kingdom are the salt of the earth. The world is dark and evil, but the citizens of His Kingdom are the light of the world. We know it's wrong to commit murder—but Jesus tells us we must not even hate. We believe in "an eye for an eye," but Jesus tells us, "Bless your enemies. Turn the other cheek." We know adultery is sin, but Jesus tells us, "If you even lust in your heart, you are already guilty."

Again and again, Jesus challenges our thinking with paradoxes and contrasts. He startles us with arresting insights. He forces us to look at the world and ourselves in new ways. He urges us to think seriously about our lives and the choices we make.

Jesus said, "Enter through the narrow gate. For wide is the gate and broad is the road that leads to destruction, and many enter through it. But small is the gate and narrow the road that leads to life, and only a few find it" (Matt. 7:13-14 NIV).

When Jesus finished delivering the Sermon on the Mount, the crowd sat in stunned amazement. They had never heard such teaching before. The other religious teachers offered opinions based on the opinions of other scholars, but Jesus spoke with authority. Jesus was a new kind of leader—and a new kind of communicator.

John 3 tells us that, one night, a man named Nicodemus came to see Jesus. This man was a powerful member of the religious ruling class, the Pharisees, and a member of the governing council, the Sanhedrin. Since the beginning of His public ministry, Jesus faced opposition from the Pharisees. Now one of the Pharisees had sought him out. Why?

Nicodemus took an enormous risk in coming to Jesus. The Pharisees had declared that anyone who followed Jesus would be banned from worshipping at the Temple. Nicodemus risked being ostracized by Jewish society in approaching Jesus this way.

Nicodemus began by saying that no one could perform the miracles Jesus did unless God was with him. Was Nicodemus sincere—or just trying to flatter Jesus? We don't know. But there was an unspoken question on this Pharisee's mind, and Jesus anticipated it: *How does a person enter the Kingdom of God?*

"Very truly," Jesus said, "I tell you, no one can see the Kingdom of God unless he is born again."

"How can someone be born when they are old? Surely they cannot enter a second time into their mother's womb to be born!"

"Very truly I tell you, no one can enter the Kingdom of God unless they are born of water and the Spirit. Flesh gives birth to flesh, but the Spirit gives birth to spirit. You should not be surprised at my saying, 'You must be born again.' The wind blows wherever it pleases. You hear its sound, but you cannot tell where it comes from or where it is going. So it is with everyone born of the Spirit."

The story of Nicodemus in John 3 ends inconclusively. There's no indication that Nicodemus made a decision that night to follow Christ. But we know that, at some point, Nicodemus became a believer. In John 19:38-40, following the crucifixion of Jesus, two men approached Pontius Pilate and ask for the crucified body of Jesus. One man was a wealthy believer named Joseph of Arimathea. The other was Nicodemus. The words of Jesus didn't change Nicodemus overnight—but they changed him.

Jesus was a great leader, in part, because he was a great communicator. He communicated Kingdom truths to vast crowds on the mountainside—and to a spiritually hungry religious leader in the dead of night. He was equally effective communicating with the masses and with the individual.

There was something about the way Jesus communicated His Kingdom vision that moved hearts and minds. The more we learn to communicate like Jesus, the more effective we will be as leaders. Here are a few of the communication principles we can learn by studying the communicating style of Jesus.

1. *Jesus seized every opportunity to communicate His Kingdom vision.*

Not long after His encounter with Nicodemus, Jesus and His disciples set off for Galilee, passing through Samaria. There, Jesus and His disciples came to the town of Sychar, located near Jacob's Well, which had been dug by the father of the Jewish people. Both the Samaritans and Jews claimed Jacob's Well as a sacred site.

Jacob's Well was fed by a spring, which people called "living water" (as opposed to the "still water" of a cistern). People had to let a clay pot into the well on a rope. When Jesus and the disciples reached Jacob's Well, they had no pot to draw water. Jesus sent his disciples into the town to buy food and He waited by the well.

What was Jesus waiting for? A drink of water? Yes, but He was also waiting for an opportunity to communicate His vision. Soon, the opportunity arrived. John 4 tells us a Samaritan woman came from town with a clay pot in her hands. As Jesus watched her approach, he prepared to give the phrase "living water" a new meaning.

Jews and Samaritans had cultural taboos that divided men from women. Jews and Samaritans also despised each other. It was unthinkable that a Jewish man would speak to a Samaritan woman. So Jesus did the unthinkable. He asked the woman for water.

She was shocked and offended. She said, "You are a Jew and I am a Samaritan woman. How can you ask me for a drink?"

"If you knew the gift of God and who it is that asks you for a drink, you would have asked him and he would have given you living water."

"Sir," the woman said (her voice must have dripped with sarcasm), "you have nothing to draw with and the well is deep. Where can you get this 'living water'? Are you greater than our father Jacob, who gave us the well and drank from it himself, as did also his sons and his livestock?"

She wasn't just asking Jesus a question. She was challenging Him and flinging her Samaritan culture and beliefs in His face. The Samaritans claimed to be true Israelites, so she was sneering at Jesus.

Jesus persisted in communicating His Kingdom vision, using the "living water" of Jacob's Well as a metaphor. "Everyone who drinks this water will be thirsty again, but whoever drinks the water I give them will never thirst. Indeed, the water I give them will become in them a spring of water welling up to eternal life."

"Sir," she said sarcastically, "give me this water so that I won't get thirsty and have to keep coming here to draw water."

Jesus said, "Go, call your husband and come back."

"I have no husband."

"You are right when you say you have no husband. The fact is, you have had five husbands, and the man you now have is not your husband. What you have just said is quite true."

"Sir," the woman said, "I can see that you are a prophet." Finally, Jesus had gotten through to her. All the mockery drained out of her voice. This stranger had just revealed the deepest secrets of her life—things He couldn't have possibly known. Finally, Jesus was able to share the good news of the Kingdom with her.

But first He had to create an opportunity. He had to ask for a drink of water.

We have dozens of opportunities every day to communicate our leadership vision, our good news, our Kingdom message. But if we are not watchful and observant, these opportunities will slip through our fingers like sand in an hourglass. To be a great communicator, watch for opportunities, make opportunities, and seize each one.

2. Jesus asked questions.

One of the most powerful ways to communicate your message is by asking questions. Throughout His ministry, Jesus asked questions that made people think. He asked rhetorical questions to make the truth stand out with clarity. He asked challenging questions to make people get off the fence and choose sides:

Speaking to crowds, He asked: If you love those who love you, what reward will you get? Who of you by worrying can add a single hour to his life? Why do you look at the speck of sawdust in your brother's eye and pay no attention to the plank in your own eye? Do people pick grapes from thornbushes, or figs from thistles?

In His clashes with the Pharisees, He asked: Why do you entertain evil thoughts in your hearts? Which is easier: to say, "Your sins are forgiven," or to say, "Get up and walk"? If any of you has a sheep and it falls into a pit on the Sabbath, will you not take hold of it and lift it out? Why do you break the command of God for the sake of your tradition? If you do not believe Moses' writings how will you believe me? Why are you angry with me for healing on the Sabbath?

He asked His disciples: Where is your faith? Do you still not understand? Who do people say the Son of Man is? Who do you say I am? What good will it be for a man if he gains the whole world, yet forfeits his soul? When the Son of Man comes, will he find faith on the earth? Who is greater, the one who is at the table or the one who serves? Don't you know me, even after I have been among you such a long time?

In his dialogues with various individuals, He asked: Why do you call me good? Which of these three do you think was a neighbor to the man who fell into the hands of robbers? Is that your own idea, or did others talk to you about me? Why are you crying? Who is it you are looking for? Do you love me?

If you want to communicate like Jesus and lead like Jesus, then learn the art of asking questions.

3. *Jesus provoked questions.*

Jesus not only asked questions, but He also stirred up questions from His followers—and His enemies. Jesus provoked questions in two ways: through his actions, and through his words.

His miracles, especially His healings, provoked the most questions. When Nicodemus came to Jesus, he said, "No one could perform the signs you are doing if God were not with him." The miracles got Nicodemus' attention, and compelled him to seek Jesus out and question Him.

You and I can't perform miracles, but we can provoke questions by the way we live our lives. Are you operating a successful business or leading an organization? Have you fought against injustice? Have you written a book or maintained a successful Internet podcast? Have you climbed a mountain, run a marathon, beaten cancer, run for public office, or lost weight? You may have a list of accomplishments I haven't even thought of. Any of these accomplishments can provoke questions from the people around you.

The words of Jesus also provoked questions. He used startling, provocative statements, such as when he told Nicodemus, "You must be born again." That strange statement riveted the attention of Nicodemus and created an opening for Jesus to share His Kingdom message in a powerful and persuasive way.

To communicate like Jesus, make statements that will leave your listeners hungering to know more. Frame your message in such a way that people can't help but ask, "What do you mean? Please tell me more!"

4. *Jesus was an excellent listener.*

Good listeners make the best communicators. When Jesus talked, He had dialogues, not monologues. When people spoke about their needs, fears, and problems, Jesus listened—and that gave him the credibility and empathy he needed to connect with people at an emotional level. People always knew he understood them. Even though he never condoned sin, he never condemned sinners. Instead, he showed them how to change their lives, and leave old sins and habits behind.

When Jesus encountered the Samaritan woman at Jacob's Well, He listened attentively. He listened as much to what she *didn't* say as to what she *did* say. He listened for her unspoken fear and guilt. He caught the unspoken meaning of her pauses and hesitations. He saw the world-weariness and desperation that clung to her.

Jesus was the greatest communicator because He was the greatest listener.

5. *Jesus was never in a hurry.*

Nicodemus came to Jesus by night—and that visit probably cost Jesus several hours of sleep. But He was never impatient, never too busy, never too tired to talk to people.

For example, instead of being too hot and tired to talk to the woman by the well, Jesus turned His thirst into a conversation-starter, and He asked her for water to drink. Jesus didn't hurry to score debating points or give his pre-rehearsed Kingdom speech. He was patient and gentle even when she was bitter and sarcastic. He gradually turned the discussion in a direction that would reveal the truths this woman needed to hear. He didn't rush, he didn't push. He was unhurried.

6. *Jesus stayed focused.*

When Nicodemus approached Jesus, he began with flattery: "Rabbi, we know that you are a teacher who has come from God." The Samaritan woman at Jacob's Well began by being combative. Jesus didn't let either flattery or hostility deflect him from His purpose. He stayed focused on communicating His Kingdom message.

In our communication opportunities, we will sometimes encounter people who want to manipulate us, distract us, change the

subject, or control the conversation. Remem
He never allowed other people to deflect hi
stayed focused.

7. *Jesus was a storyteller.*

He used stories called "parables" to ill
Matthew's gospel contains a series of parable ~~jesus told a crowd by~~
a lake. Matthew makes a surprising statement: "Jesus spoke all these
things to the crowd in parables; he did not say anything to them
without using a parable" (Matt. 13:34 NIV). Isn't that amazing? He
didn't lecture or engage in soaring oratory. He told stories.

The parables of Jesus were simple stories on the surface, but
contained depths of meaning that seemed to go on forever. His
stories frequently included surprise twists that challenged the hearer
to think more deeply, to set aside preconceived notions, and discover
a new perspective.

Jesus used stories to make his teachings vivid and unforgettable.
"The best way to learn is through stories," said leadership teacher
Ken Blanchard. "I know that because of the way people respond to
my stories in my lectures. Stories permit the audience and readers to
identify and get into the characters and learn right along with the
characters. It makes learning effortless and enjoyable."[4] When I'm
speaking to an audience, if I notice people checking their phones or
nodding off, I use a phrase guaranteed to make them sit up straight:
"Let me tell you a story...."

Jesus didn't use stories merely to get his listeners' attention. His
parables conveyed truth. These stories spoke for themselves, and were
designed to produce a sudden flash of insight. Instead of telling us,
"God loves you and He wants to welcome you no matter how far
you've strayed from His will," Jesus told us the story of Prodigal Son
and the Loving Father.

d like Jesus, let's communicate like Jesus. Let's seize every
unity, ask questions, provoke questions, listen, be available
d unhurried, and stay focused. Above all, let's be storytellers.

JESUS, THE MASTER OF PEOPLE SKILLS

No one ever had greater people skills than Jesus. He used a three-step leadership model: mentoring, training, and delegating. He began by calling the disciples to Himself and investing His life in them. Then he trained them and taught them to preach the message of the Kingdom. Finally, He delegated His authority to them and sent them out to minister in His name.

By mentoring, training, and delegating His ministry to the Twelve, Jesus reproduced Himself eleven times over (Judas, of course, was an exception to this rule). Jesus didn't simply clone Himself. He mentored and trained each disciple according to his own uniqueness. No two disciples were alike. Two thousand years later, the leadership model of Jesus is still God's chosen model for the church. God continues to multiply His followers and expand His kingdom through the leadership model of Jesus.

When the people you lead fail you or disappoint you, when they betray you or hurt you, it's only natural to be angry. That's when you need the people skills of Jesus. Most people think of Jesus as only getting angry once—when He drove the moneychangers out of the temple. But Jesus was angry quite a number of times—and of course, His anger was always a righteous anger.

In Mark 3, Jesus is in the synagogue on the Sabbath. A man is brought before Him with a shriveled hand, and the religious leaders watch to see what Jesus will do. They claim it's sin to do any work, even healing, on the Sabbath. Jesus knows they are plotting to kill

Him, so He says, "Which is lawful on the Sabbath—to do good or to do evil, to save life or to kill?"

Then, Mark writes, Jesus "looked around at them in anger," being "deeply distressed at their stubborn hearts." Then he healed the man's shriveled hand. God commanded that people keep the Sabbath holy, but the corrupt religious leaders had added hundreds of rules to God's simple command. Jesus was angry not only with their murderous intentions, but with their irrational insistence that man-made rules should come before doing good.

Human anger tends to harden into grudges, bitterness, and hate. But the anger of Jesus always produced healthy, constructive action. In Mark 10, people bring children to Jesus, asking Him to bless them and pray for them—but the disciples, thinking Jesus is too busy for little children, shoo these families away. When Jesus sees what His disciples are doing, He becomes "indignant" and He says, "Let the little children come to me, and do not hinder them, for the Kingdom of Heaven belongs to such as these." Jesus is a Friend to children, and His command to His disciples is a word of rebuke.

There were other times when Jesus was displeased with his disciples. Once, when the disciples tried and failed to heal a boy afflicted by an evil spirit, Jesus said, "You unbelieving generation! How long shall I stay with you? How long shall I put up with you?"

In *The Emotions of Jesus*, Robert Law asks: Where does the anger of Jesus come from? He writes:

> The answer to that question is evident. God is love; Jesus is love; the anger of Jesus and all holy anger is the anger of love. For love is not wholly sympathy and sweetness; love is full of indignation and wrath. When you see someone maltreating a child, what happens? Your sympathy with the

child instantly becomes wrath against his persecutor and rises up in arms against him. You love your own child, you fervently desire his highest good, and what would your love be worth if it did not inspire you with wrath against anyone seeking to undermine his purity and teach him the pleasures of sin?[5]

As we follow Jesus, we need to make sure our anger is a loving anger, a protective and righteous anger that brings healing, not hurt. It must be a selfless anger, never a selfish anger. Jesus was never angry over insults and injustices against Himself. When He was flogged and beaten and mocked and spat upon, He didn't become angry. He loved and forgave His enemies. As Max Lucado wrote, "Nails didn't hold Jesus to the cross; love did."

There are a number of people skills we need in our daily leadership lives: the skill of loving others unconditionally, the skill of forgiving our followers when they fail, the skill of empathizing with others, the skill of protecting our followers' reputations, the skill of being patient with our followers, the skill of inspiring and motivating our followers, and the skill of managing our anger. Jesus had these people skills in abundance.

Few of us are born with the people skills we need to be leaders. The good news is that all of these skills can be learned and improved through practice.

JESUS, THE LEADER OF CHARACTER

Jesus possessed an array of character traits that enabled him to impact and influence others, earn the trust of his followers, and become the most effective leader in history. Let's look at a few of the character traits of Jesus—traits you and I can study and emulate:

First, *Jesus had compassion for people.* Matthew's gospel tells us, "When he saw the crowds, he had compassion on them, because they were harassed and helpless, like sheep without a shepherd" (Matt. 9:36 NIV). His heart was broken over the needs of others.

Second, *Jesus had an unshakable commitment to his mission in life.* He was aware of his calling—and He was focused on completing His mission. He knew He had come to die as a sacrifice for our sin. He knew that the cross stood in His path, and He had to pass through the door of torture, death, and separation from the Father. Even so, He completed His mission. Commitment is a key character trait for leadership.

Third, *Jesus had perfect self-control.* Before Jesus began His public ministry, He was led by the Spirit into the desert to be tempted. Satan offered Him food, power, and kingdoms—yet Jesus maintained His self-control. He subordinated His human desires to a far greater desire to serve God. We all need self-control to achieve our leadership goals.

Fourth, *Jesus possessed absolute humility.* His was not a false humility. He didn't deny who He was—the Messiah, the Son of the living God—but He didn't use His power to serve Himself. He served others at the expense of Himself. If you want to know what humility looks like, study the life of Jesus.

Fifth, *Jesus was a role model of gentleness.* He could be angry in the face of injustice, but when people were hurting, when sinners repented, when children were placed in His arms, He was the gentlest human being on the planet. We sometimes forget that people need a leader's gentle touch.

Sixth, *Jesus possessed patience.* He was patient with the doubts, failings, and misunderstandings of the disciples. He maintained his composure and responded patiently to every person he spoke to.

Seventh, *Jesus was prayerful*. No matter how busy He was, Jesus made time to be alone with God in prayer. He never let the pressures of His public ministry divert Him from His priority of spending time alone with the Father.

Jesus proved the importance of good character as a leadership asset. People willingly follow leaders who build trust on a foundation of good character.

JESUS, THE COMPETENT LEADER

A competent leader possesses the skills, behaviors, and attitudes that lead the organization to success. Jesus schooled himself in the Scriptures from an early age. When He was only twelve, He debated the learned rabbis of Jerusalem and astonished them with His knowledge.

As a man of thirty, Jesus demonstrated all the skills that a leader needs. He was competent to speak persuasively and compellingly before crowds. He was competent to teach and train His disciples. He was competent to delegate authority and tasks to his followers, and hold them accountable for the results.

At the outset of His ministry, Jesus did all the preaching, teaching, healing, and driving out demons by Himself. In effect, He said, "I'll work, you watch." In the middle stages of His ministry, Jesus involved His followers and let them gain hands-on experience. In effect, He said, "I'll work, you help." Gradually, Jesus transferred responsibility to their shoulders so that, when the time came for Him to leave them, they would be ready to take over. Ultimately, He was able to say, "You work, I'll watch."

Jesus promised the Twelve that they would achieve even greater things than He had. He built their confidence and taught them His Kingdom message. They, in turn, taught others. Generation by generation, the message spread and the church grew and grew. Today, I am a twenty-first century follower of Jesus, and so are you. We are living evidence of the leadership competence of Jesus, because the movement He started twenty centuries ago is still attracting followers today.

JESUS, THE BOLD LEADER

Jesus was the boldest leader of all time. There is no more bold and courageous act of leadership than to lay down your life for your followers. Jesus demonstrated bold leadership from the beginning of His ministry until the day He left this earth.

He boldly drove the moneychangers out of the Temple to cleanse it of corruption. He boldly opposed the religious rulers even though He knew they were plotting to kill Him. He boldly confronted Pontius Pilate, the Roman governor, even though this man had the power to have Him crucified.

Jesus called His followers to live boldly and dare to do the impossible. He walked on water—then He boldly called Peter to step out of the boat and do the impossible as well. If you are a leader, then part of your job is to motivate and inspire your followers to dare to do the impossible. Call them out of the safety of their snug little boat and send them out upon the churning waters of uncertainty.

To lead like Jesus, live boldly like Jesus.

JESUS, THE SERVANT LEADER

Jesus showed us that an authentic leader has a serving heart. He didn't come into the world to be served. He came as a servant to others. Paul described His serving heart this way:

In your relationships with one another, have the same mindset as Christ Jesus:

Who, being in very nature God,
    did not consider equality with God something to be
    used to his own advantage;
rather, he made himself nothing
    by taking the very nature of a servant,
    being made in human likeness.
And being found in appearance as a man,
    he humbled himself
    by becoming obedient to death—
      even death on a cross! (Phil. 2:5-8 NIV)

The most dramatic demonstration of the serving heart of Jesus took place in the hours before He went to the cross. He and His disciples were in the upper room, sharing a last meal together. After three years of walking with Jesus, His disciples still didn't understand His Kingdom message. They argued among themselves about which of them would be the greatest in His Kingdom.

Jesus sat quietly and sadly, listening to their bickering. They were His friends, and He loved them—and He was leaving them behind to carry out the revolution of love. Now He had one last lesson to teach them. He stood and left the table, removed his robe, took a pitcher and poured water into a basin, and wrapped a towel around His waist. Then He took the basin and towel and began washing the disciples' feet.

As Jesus demonstrated his serving heart to the disciples, their voices fell silent. Every eye was on Jesus. He went from one man to the next to the next, washing the feet of the Twelve, including Judas, who would betray him.

Then Jesus told them why He washed their feet. "You call me 'Teacher' and 'Lord,'" Jesus said, "and rightly so, for that is what I am. Now that I, your Lord and Teacher, have washed your feet, you also should wash one another's feet. I have set you an example that you should do as I have done for you" (John 13:13-15 NIV).

Max Lucado explains what this act means in our lives today. "Jesus kneels down and gazes upon the darkest acts of our lives," he writes. "But rather than recoil in horror, he reaches out in kindness and says, 'I can clean that if you want.' And from the basin of his grace, he scoops a palm full of mercy and washes our sin."[6]

Pastor Rick Warren of Saddleback Church in California points out that there have been thousands of books written on leadership, but very few on servanthood. The reason? "Everyone wants to lead; no one wants to be a servant." It's true. Bosses get the praise and the big money. Servants get the grunt work. Jesus showed us by His example that we should aspire to take up the basin and the towel. We should wash feet.

No leader in human history was ever more deserving to be called "great" than Jesus—and none was more humble. Jesus set aside His authority and His right to rule the universe, and He became a suffering servant. He demonstrated a kind of leadership the world had never seen before.

Only leaders who serve should serve as leaders.

CHAPTER 1: QUESTIONS FOR REFLECTION AND DISCUSSION

1. As Christians, we believe that Jesus is the Messiah, the Son of God—literally God in human form. We can't possess the attributes of God. In what ways, then, can Jesus be our role model of leadership?

2. Describe a time when you led like Jesus, consciously following His leadership example. What was the result?

   Or describe a time when you *should* have led like Jesus, but didn't. What was the result?

3. Jesus mentored and trained twelve disciples, one of whom betrayed Him. Through the remaining eleven, He changed the world. What does the example of Jesus suggest to you about your own leadership and mentoring strategy? What lessons can you learn from His interactions with the Twelve that can make you a more effective leader?

4. What are the communication skills and methods Jesus used to be such an effective and persuasive communicator? What lessons can you learn from His example to become a more effective communicator?

5. How did Jesus's serving heart make Him more effective as a leader? What steps can you take in your leadership life—in your home, your church, your office, or your team—to become a better servant leader?

6. Jesus was the ultimate leader, complete in all Seven Sides of Leadership—Vision, Communication, People Skills, Good Character, Competence, Boldness, and A Serving Heart. In which of these leadership attributes do you most need to grow?

   What steps can you take to lead more like Jesus in that one leadership attribute?

CHAPTER 2

SAMUEL, AMOS, AND DANIEL: THREE LEADERS OF VISION

Twenty-three-year-old Henry Ford lived with his new bride in a log cabin he had built with his own hands. He was a machinist and a farmer with a fully equipped workshop behind his cabin where he sometimes built hand-made steam engines for trucks and tractors.

One day in 1885, a man from Eagle Iron Works in Detroit came to Ford's farm and asked him if he could repair an Otto gasoline-powered engine. Ford had never seen one before, but he confidently told the man he could get it running. He went to the iron factory and tore into the engine, figuring out how it worked as he went. By the time he got it back together, he was an expert on the internal combustion engine.

That day, Henry Ford had a vision of a future America in which thousands of gasoline-powered cars would be on the roads, taking people and goods across the nation. He went to work, designing a car that would run on gasoline, be easy to maintain, and be affordable to all. Eventually, he designed a vehicle called the Model A, and his company turned out fifteen cars a day. That company became known as the Ford Motor Company.

It all began with a vision in the mind of a twenty-three-year-old machinist.

Now, I'm not saying that the vision Henry Ford had is the same kind of vision God gave the Old Testament prophets. But as we look at the lives of the prophets, we will discover insights and lessons we can apply to our leadership lives.

A vision is a word-picture that leaders use to motivate and inspire their people and move them to toward a desired goal. Vision is the first of The Seven Sides of Leadership. The reason vision comes first is that everything starts with the leader's vision, and everything flows from that vision.

Our vision of the future determines the goals we must set in order to achieve success. The leader's vision paints the target so that everyone in the organization knows exactly where they are headed and why. A vision is aspirational and inspirational—it fills the heart of every person with a sense of mission and purpose.

Thousands of years ago, God entrusted divinely inspired visions to certain specially chosen individuals known as prophets. A prophet proclaims the message of God to the people. In this chapter, we're going to look at a few selected Old Testament prophets and discover the lessons we can learn for our own leadership lives.

In Old Testament times, a vision was information that God supernaturally gave His prophets concerning the future. Often that information was conditional: serve and obey God, and you will be blessed—rebel and disobey God and you will suffer the consequences.

A vision should be clear and simple. In the Old Testament, God said, "Write down the revelation and make it plain on tablets so that a herald may run with it" (Hab. 2:2 NIV). Or, as *The Message* translation renders this verse, "Write this. Write what you see. Write it out in big block letters so that it can be read on the run." Make your vision clear and communicate it simply.

Often the information God revealed through His prophets was quite specific, as when God revealed to Jeremiah that Israel would be invaded by Babylon and be taken into captivity for seventy years (Jer. 25:9-11 NIV). God may not give you and me such specific and dramatic visions today, but we should still seek His leading in our daily prayers and Bible study. We should constantly listen for His voice, so that we can align our leadership priorities with His will.

SAMUEL: FIRST OF THE PROPHETS

Samuel's life straddled the dividing line between two distinct eras in Israel's history, the time of the Judges and the time of the Kingdom of Israel. There was no central government in Israel from the time Joshua led the conquest of the Promised Land until the birth of Samuel. The tribes of Israel were loosely affiliated, and would sometimes band together against a common enemy—when they weren't squabbling with each other.

Throughout the Book of Judges, we see a cyclical pattern in which the people of Israel would gradually slip into apostasy and idolatry. They would adopt the sinful practices of the surrounding pagan nations. To discipline the Israelites and bring them to their senses, God would send a pagan nation to oppress them. In their suffering, the people would cry out to God for deliverance—and God would hear their cry and raise up a judge to deliver the Israelites in their time of need. The Book of Judges describes the actions of twelve of these judges, ending with Samson.

In 1 Samuel, we meet the successor of Samson, the last of the Old Testament judges and first of the Old Testament prophets, Samuel. He would not only judge Israel as the other judges had done, but he would speak God's prophetic vision to Israel. He offered sacrifices to

God on behalf of the people, which made him a priest as well. Later, Samuel would also anoint the first two kings of Israel, King Saul and King David.

For years before Samuel was born, his mother Hannah was unable to conceive. In desperation and despair, she vowed that if God would give her a child, she would dedicate the child to God. Soon afterward, Hannah conceived and gave birth to Samuel. True to her vow, she placed the boy in the care of Eli, the priest of Shiloh. There Samuel served Eli and was taught and trained by him.

The third chapter of 1 Samuel contains a tragic statement: "In those days the word of the Lord was rare; *there were not many visions*" (1 Sam. 3:1b NIV). In other words, God was silent in those days. The nation received no word from Him about the future. The people had no sense of national purpose. There was no vision in the land, and because there was no vision, there was no moral and spiritual leadership in the nation.

One night when Samuel was a young boy, God broke His silence. Samuel was in bed when he heard a voice calling his name. He thought Eli was calling, so he got up and went to Eli to ask what he wanted. Eli hadn't called him, so he told the boy to go back to sleep. This happened three times. Finally, Eli realized it was God Himself who called to Samuel, and he told Samuel to reply, "Speak, Lord, for your servant is listening." Samuel did as Eli told him, and the Lord told Samuel that the two sons of Eli were wicked and Eli had failed to restrain them. Therefore, God was going to punish Eli and his sons.

The next morning, Samuel was reluctant to report the message to Eli, but Eli told Samuel to tell him everything God had said. Samuel told Eli everything. Then Eli said, "He is the Lord; let Him do what is good in His eyes." God had given Samuel a vision of a tragic future for Eli and his sons, and Samuel faithfully delivered that vision to Eli.

After this incident, there's a fascinating statement in 1 Samuel 3:19—"The Lord was with Samuel as he grew up, and he let none of Samuel's words fall to the ground." God entrusted a crucial message to Samuel, and because Samuel had been faithful in delivering God's message to Eli, He entrusted Samuel with many other important messages over the years. Samuel spoke God's truth. He delivered God's message. And God never let any of Samuel's words be wasted. All of Samuel's words were important.

This incident, in which God literally called the boy Samuel by name, was the moment Samuel became the first of God's Old Testament prophets. In the New Testament, both the apostle Peter in Acts 3:24 and the apostle Paul in Acts 13:20 identify Samuel as the last of the Old Testament judges and the first of the prophets. The Scriptures tell us that "all Israel from Dan to Beersheba recognized that Samuel was attested as a prophet of the Lord. The Lord continued to appear at Shiloh, and there he revealed himself to Samuel through his word" (1 Sam. 3:20-21 NIV).

Samuel was probably ten years old when he received this first vision from the Lord. Two decades later, when Samuel was about thirty, the Israelites went to war against the Philistines. They took the Ark of the Covenant out of the tabernacle in Shiloh and carried it into battle against the Philistines. During the battle, Eli's sons were killed, just as God had foretold to Samuel—and the Ark was captured by the pagan enemy.

A fleeing Israelite soldier reached Shiloh and told Eli that his two sons had been killed in battle, and the Ark had been seized by the Philistines. Hearing this news, ninety-eight-year-old Eli fell backwards, broke his neck, and died.

God chose Samuel to succeed Eli as the leader of the Israelite people. As a judge and prophet over Israel, Samuel succeeded in turning the idolatrous people back to the one true God. Then he led the Israelite army to victory over the Philistines at Mizpah. Samuel won the victory not by military strategy or superior weaponry, but by sacrificing a lamb (representing the future sacrifice of Jesus on the cross) and by continual prayer. God sent the bone-shaking roar of thunder against the Philistines, causing them to flee in panic. The Israelites chased the Philistines and slaughtered them, ending four decades of threats, sneak attacks, and terrorism.

Samuel set up a stone monument as a reminder of the victory God had given to Israel. He called the stone "Ebenezer," which means, "Thus far the Lord has helped us." If you have heard the old hymn, "Come Thou Fount of Every Blessing," you may have been puzzled by a line in the song that says, "Here I raise my Ebenezer." That line refers to the monument Samuel set up after Israel's triumph over the Philistines.

Following this victory, Israel enjoyed peace throughout the rest of Samuel's life. Samuel built an altar to the Lord at Shiloh, and founded a school for prophets at Ramah.

Though Samuel maintained his integrity throughout his life, his sons became corrupt and extorted bribes from the people. The people of Israel said to Samuel, "You are old, and your sons do not follow your ways. Now appoint a king to lead us, such as all the other nations have."

Angry and discouraged, Samuel prayed and God told him, "Listen to all that the people are saying to you. It is not you they have rejected, but they have rejected me as their King" (1 Sam. 8:1-9 NIV).

Samuel reluctantly agreed to anoint Israel's first king, a man named Saul (1 Sam. 10 NIV). Saul proved to be unstable and disobedient to God, so Samuel anointed Israel's second king, King David (1 Sam. 16:13 NIV). When Samuel died, the nation of Israel mourned him and buried him at his home in Ramah (1 Sam. 25:1 NIV).

The achievements of Samuel are nothing short of amazing. At the time of his birth, Israel was a loose and fragmented collection of tribes. Their worship was polluted by idolatry. They were constantly being raided and terrorized by the Philistines. God used Samuel to bring about enormous change in the life of the nation.

By the end of Samuel's life, Israel was restored as a godly nation, united under Samuel's leadership. The people had a strong sense of national purpose and a vision of what their nation could be if they would obey God. Samuel reminded the Israelites that God had chosen Israel to reflect the light of His power and wisdom to the nations.

More than any other prophet in the Old Testament, Samuel promoted the idea that worship meant more than following rituals and sacrifices. It meant seeking an intimate relationship with God, loving Him and obeying Him.

Why did Samuel have such a dramatic impact on the nation of Israel? I believe it's because, when God called young Samuel, he obediently replied, "Speak, Lord, for your servant is listening." Samuel was ready to receive the vision God wanted to give him. There were not many visions given among the people in those days, because there were not many people who were receptive to God's call. Samuel's willing, waiting, listening attitude made all the difference.

What are the lessons we can learn from the visionary leadership of Samuel?

FIRST LESSON: *Never assume that visionary leadership belongs only to the old.*

Samuel was too young to realize it, but the moment he began to listen for God's voice, he became a visionary leader in Israel. God could have spoken directly to Eli, but He chose to entrust this vision to a little boy. I think He had at least two reasons for doing so.

I believe God knew this vision would have more impact coming from the trembling lips of a boy than from God's own thundering voice. I think God was saying to Eli, "You've failed to restrain the wickedness of your sons. Therefore, I am transferring the mantle of visionary leadership from you to young Samuel."

Also, God was teaching Samuel an early lesson in how to be a visionary leader. It is never too early to train young people to be leaders of vision who listen for God's voice.

SECOND LESSON: *When God gives you a vision, don't hold back—communicate it.*

Don't waste words, don't waste time, don't let your words fall to the ground. Get to the point, communicate your vision, make your words count.

This was a leadership lesson Samuel learned at a tender young age. When God gave a vision to young Samuel about Eli, Samuel was afraid to speak it out loud. Though Eli had failed to raise godly sons, he did raise Samuel to be a godly leader. So Eli persuaded Samuel to speak God's truth without hesitation. It was a leadership lesson Samuel never forgot.

THIRD LESSON: *To be a leader of vision, listen for the voice of the Lord.*

Don't concoct a vision of your own, then ask God to bless it. Listen and wait for God to send you a vision straight from His heart. When He calls you, let your response be, "Speak, Lord, for your servant is listening." Then follow the vision He gives you wherever it leads.

FOURTH LESSON: *When God gives you success, celebrate His triumph in a visible, memorable way.*

Raise a monument, an "Ebenezer" of praise to God, when He gives you a victory—and especially when you successfully achieve your vision by God's grace. Put a bronze plaque on the wall, hang a banner from the rafters of your arena, post a video to your company website, or name a building "Ebenezer Hall." Make sure that whenever people pass that monument or click on that website, they remember God's triumph and continue to celebrate it with thanks to God.

Samuel's life teaches us that those who listen for the Lord's voice will see visions. When God gives you His vision, it will not only change your life—it will change everything.

AMOS: THE THUNDERING SHEPHERD

The prophet Amos lived around the same time as Isaiah and Hosea. He was born in the southern Kingdom of Judah, but preached and prophesied in the northern Kingdom of Israel. He emerged during a time when the Israelites were neglecting God and His laws. There was poverty and injustice in the land. The prophecies of Amos were largely an indictment of Israel's lack of compassion for the poor at that time.

Amos made it clear that he was not a professional prophet, and was not trained in Samuel's school for prophets. He said, "I was neither a prophet nor the son of a prophet, but I was a shepherd, and I also took care of sycamore-fig trees." The phrase "son of a prophet" does not refer to his parentage; a "son of a prophet" was someone who had been trained as a prophet. He added, "But the Lord took me from tending the flock and said to me, 'Go, prophesy to my people Israel'" (Amos 7:14-15 NIV).

Amos established his credentials as a true prophet by saying that he was not a trained professional prophet. He was a simple shepherd, minding his own business, when God tapped him on the shoulder and called him to prophesy. Amos prophesied against the wicked nations surrounding Israel—and then he prophesied against Israel itself.

In chapters 3 through 6, Amos charged Israel with sin and declared God's judgment against Israel. He indicted Israel's ruling class for turning from God to false idols, living extravagantly on the backs of the poor, and corrupting justice. God had judged Israel, and would send an enemy from the north to sweep down and take the Israelites captive.

A key passage of Amos deals with justice for the poor and oppressed (this was a favorite verse of Dr. Martin Luther King, Jr.): "But let justice roll on like a river, righteousness like a never-failing stream!" (Amos 5:24 NIV). Amos not only saw visions, but he communicated in visionary language, rich in metaphors.

Jeroboam II was King of Israel in Amos's day. He reigned nearly eight hundred years before Christ. His army defeated the Arameans and conquered Damascus. In 1910, archaeologists excavating the royal palace in Samaria found pieces of broken pottery with inscriptions that tell of the reign of Jeroboam II, confirming the Old Testament accounts.

The rich vineyards and olive groves of Israel produced wine and oil the Israelites traded with other nations. As a result, Israel enjoyed enormous prosperity. Israelite merchants and government officials owned palaces and lived in luxury and splendor—yet they were boastful, arrogant, and selfish. They exploited the poor and had no compassion for the oppressed.

Idol worship was a spiritual cancer in Israel. Jeroboam II established shrines to false gods, with obscene rituals and practices. Three

Old Testament prophets spoke out against the sins of Jeroboam—
Hosea, Joel, and Amos. The prophet Amos thundered God's
judgment against Israel in vivid terms:

> You lie on beds adorned with ivory
>> and lounge on your couches.
> You dine on choice lambs
>> and fattened calves.
> You strum away on your harps like David
>> and improvise on musical instruments.
> You drink wine by the bowlful
>> and use the finest lotions,
>>> but you do not grieve over the ruin of Joseph.
> Therefore you will be among the first to go into exile;
>> your feasting and lounging will end.

> The Sovereign Lord has sworn by himself—the Lord God
> Almighty declares:

> "I abhor the pride of Jacob
>> and detest his fortresses;
> I will deliver up the city
>> and everything in it." (Amos 6:4-8 NIV)

In Amos 7, the shepherd prophet describes three visions God
gave him. God first shows Amos that He is preparing swarms
of locusts to consume the land. Amos cries out, "Sovereign Lord,
forgive! How can Jacob survive? He is so small!" ("Jacob," of course,
is Amos's poetic term for the nation of Israel, because the patriarch
Jacob was the father of Israel.) God responds to Amos's plea, saying,
"This will not happen."

In the second vision, God shows Amos that He is preparing a fire to consume the land. Again, Amos cries out, "Sovereign Lord, I beg you, stop! How can Jacob survive? He is so small!" And God says, "This will not happen either."

In the third vision, however, there are no swarms of locusts, no consuming fire. The image is calm and commonplace. The Lord stands next to a wall and holds a plumb line in his hand. A plumb line is a builder's tool, a string with a lead weight attached to the end. Suspend a plumb line at a height of several feet above the ground, and it will form a straight vertical line. The weight (or "plumb") will obey gravity and draw the string taut toward the center of the earth.

God stands next to a wall, measuring to see if the wall is straight. He asks the shepherd prophet, "What do you see, Amos?"

"A plumb line."

"Look, I am setting a plumb line among my people Israel; I will spare them no longer."

God is measuring the hearts of the people to see whose heart is upright—and whose is bent away from God. He will punish those whose heart is "out of plumb." God says to Amos: "The high places of Isaac will be destroyed and the sanctuaries of Israel will be ruined; with my sword I will rise against the house of Jeroboam."

Amos had no official leadership position in Israel. He was not even a subject of the northern kingdom. He came from the southern kingdom of Judah. So he was *persona non grata* in Israel, a nobody, without any official leadership role.

Yet God had commissioned him to take a vision of the future to the nation of Israel. Amos was a leader because God said so. When God taps you and says, "Lead," it's time to step up and lead.

Amos is often depicted as a harsh, take-no-prisoners prophet who thundered God's judgment. But Amos was also a deeply compassionate man who cared about the poor and oppressed. When God revealed these visions to Amos, the prophet had compassion for the Israelites—or "Jacob," as he called them. He said, "Sovereign Lord, forgive! How can Jacob survive? He is so small!"

Great leaders have compassion for their people. A leader without compassion is a tyrant.

After Amos pleaded for mercy, God agreed not to impose the first two punishments—the locusts and the fire. Amos was a farmer, and he knew a locust swarm would devastate the food supply and cause starvation in Israel. God was prepared to launch a direct attack against the prosperity of Israel because the nation had rejected God.

Locusts are short-horned grasshoppers that have a swarming phase. Locusts attack fruits and vegetables, including grapes and olives, the primary exports of Israel (in the form of wine and olive oil). In March through October 1915, the land of Palestine was devastated by swarms of locusts. Photographs of that plague show wheat fields stripped to the bare earth, olive trees covered with millions of locusts, and vineyards denuded of leaves and fruit. Most farmers lost everything. Scarcity sent prices soaring—$15 for a sack of flour, and sugar could not be bought at any price.

Jewish leaders in Palestine called for a time of Taanit Tzibbur, a communal period of prayer and fasting. Within days after the Taanit Tzibbur, the plague of locusts ended. Some say the locusts left because they had finished feeding, but others believed God had answered their prayer.

Like swarms of locusts, a raging fire can destroy the wealth of the land. When fire rages out of control, it leaves nothing standing. Amos again pleaded for the nation, and his two prayers revealed the heart of Amos—the heart of a compassionate, godly leader: "How can Jacob survive? He is so small!"

God responded to Amos's prayer. He didn't change his mind about the Israelites' sin, but He showed mercy and grace to Israel. God doesn't want to punish His children—yet when we force His hand, He will do what He must to get our attention.

But Amos had a third vision—the vision of the plumb line. This vision tells us that God uses a moral and spiritual plumb line to measure the uprightness of His people. "Look," God tells Amos, "I am setting a plumb line among my people Israel; I will spare them no longer." Twice before, God has responded to the prayer of Amos, but the judgment of the plumb line is not like the first two judgments.

The judgments of locusts and fire would have been general and indiscriminate. Everyone in Israel would have suffered, rich and poor, righteous and wicked. But the plumb line judgment is selective and precisely measured. God is lowering a plumb line to measure the heart of every individual. He is going to objectively know who is upright and who is not. In this judgment, the arrogant and ungodly will be punished—and the righteous will be spared. God tells Amos:

The high places of Isaac will be destroyed
and the sanctuaries of Israel will be ruined;
with my sword I will rise against the house of
Jeroboam. (Amos 7:9 NIV)

The "high places" are the mountaintop shrines where the unfaithful people of Israel had set up idols. The sanctuaries are the temples that were originally established for the worship of God, but were later used for the worship of idols. These were also the gathering places for the high and mighty, the corrupt oppressors of the poor. In these high places and sanctuaries, the rich and powerful people of Israelite society flaunted their wealth. God said He would destroy those places—and King Jeroboam II would be punished "with my sword." In other words, an enemy nation would invade Israel, and it would be like a sword in God's hand to punish the godless king.

After the third vision, Amos didn't pray for God to be merciful. He knew God's judgment was just, and His punishment would be meted out to those who had earned it.

In chapter 8, God shows Amos another vision—a vision of a basket of ripe fruit. God explains: "The time is ripe for my people Israel; I will spare them no longer." The first ten verses of chapter 9 continue God's vivid prophecy of the destruction of wayward, sinful Israel—but again, we see that God's judgment is righteous and just, because he tells Amos:

> "Yet I will not totally destroy
>   the descendants of Jacob,"
>   declares the Lord.
> "For I will give the command,
>   and I will shake the people of Israel
>   among all the nations
> as grain is shaken in a sieve,
>   and not a pebble will reach the ground.
> All the sinners among my people
>   will die by the sword,
> all those who say,
>   'Disaster will not overtake or meet us.'"
>   (Amos 9:8b-10 NIV)

The prophecy was not fulfilled immediately. The Lord gave the Israelites time to repent. Then, about fifteen years after this prophecy, the Assyrians under Tiglath-Pileser III invaded the northern kingdom and took the leaders of the nation into captivity, as described in 1 Chronicles 5:26 and 2 Kings 15:29. A decade or so later, the Assyrians under Sargon II and his son Shalmaneser V attacked Israel again, laid siege to the capital city for three years, and carried off thousands of captives. The Scriptures tell us:

> The king of Assyria deported Israel to Assyria and settled them in Halah, in Gozan on the Habor River and in towns of the Medes. This happened because they had not obeyed the Lord their God, but had violated his covenant—all that Moses the servant of the Lord commanded. They neither listened to the commands nor carried them out. (2 Kings 18:11–12 NIV)

Those who had once enjoyed wealth and privilege became slaves in a barbarian land. They lost their Jewish language and religion, and they melted into the pagan culture. Today, the Israelites who were captured by Assyria are known as the Ten Lost Tribes of Israel.

The prophecy of Amos tells us the righteous have nothing to fear from God's judgment. In fact, the last five verses of Amos give us a vision of a bright future for those who remain faithful to God:

> "In that day
>
>> I will restore David's fallen shelter—
>>> I will repair its broken walls
>>> and restore its ruins—
>>> and will rebuild it as it used to be,
>> so that they may possess the remnant of Edom
>>> and all the nations that bear my name,"
>>>> declares the Lord, who will do these things.
>
> "The days are coming," declares the Lord,
>
>> "when the reaper will be overtaken by the plowman

and the planter by the one treading grapes.
New wine will drip from the mountains
    and flow from all the hills,
    and I will bring my people Israel back from exile.
"They will rebuild the ruined cities and live in them.
    They will plant vineyards and drink their wine;
    they will make gardens and eat their fruit.
I will plant Israel in their own land,
    never again to be uprooted
    from the land I have given them,"

    says the Lord your God. (Amos 9:11-15 NIV)

Though the Book of Amos is filled with dire prophecies of judgment and destruction, God ultimately gives us a vision of hope. The walls will be restored, new wine will flow from the vineyards, and the gardens will be lush with fruit. What are the lessons we can learn from the visionary example of Amos?

FIRST LESSON: *Leadership starts with a vision, and sometimes it is a two-sided vision.*

When a team, a church, an organization, or a nation falls away from the right path, the leader must cast a vision of two alternative futures: "Here is a vision of the consequences of disobedience. And here is a vision of the rewards of faithfulness. We will decide which vision becomes our reality." Amos presented such a two-sided vision. Tragically, Israel chose self-destruction.

SECOND LESSON: *Sometimes outsiders bring the clearest vision to a situation.*

Amos was an outsider, a man of the southern kingdom, Judah. He was also an outsider to the ruling class, a lowly shepherd and a farmer.

Yet God sent Amos the Outsider to confront the sins of the king and the ruling class. Amos the Outsider saw clearly how depraved the nation had become. The king and his advisers couldn't see the problem. They were neck-deep in sin and idolatry—and they felt satisfied with their way of life. This ignorant peasant from Judah had nothing to say to them. Yet God was foretelling their future through Amos the Outsider.

Don't hesitate to share your vision, simply because you are an outsider. You may have the clearest view of the truth.

THIRD LESSON: *A leader of vision must be impartial.*

God demonstrates the absolute impartiality of His judgment when He gives Amos the vision of the plumb line. In the process, God shows Amos that a leader, too, must be impartial. A plumb line is unbiased because it is calibrated by the force of gravity. It cannot give a false reading. If a wall or a column does not align with a plumb line, you can be certain the plumb line is not at fault. It is the workmanship that is defective.

God makes a "plumb line" measurement of the human heart. His standard is unbiased and accurate. As leaders, we must sometimes challenge and correct our followers—and we must do so without favoritism.

Impartiality doesn't mean treating everyone the same. It means treating everyone fairly. If you have two employees, one lazy and another industrious, it would be unfair to treat them the same. To be impartial, treat everyone as an individual, according to what they contribute to the team. Make room for mercy, as God did. Allow people to repent and be restored. Cultivate a reputation for fairness. As a visionary leader, always keep your plumb line handy.

FOURTH LESSON: *Always be fired up with urgency and enthusiasm.*

Dr. Martin Luther King, Jr., once gave a speech known as the "Mountaintop Speech," in which he spoke in eloquent, visionary terms of the future of the civil rights movement. Dr. King used the prophet Amos as a role model for how civil rights leaders and preachers should deliver the message of freedom and justice to the world. He said:

> Who is it that is supposed to articulate the longings and aspirations of the people more than the preacher? Somehow the preacher must have a kind of fire shut up in his bones. And whenever injustice is around he tells it. Somehow the preacher must be an Amos, and saith, "When God speaks who can but prophesy?" Again with Amos, "Let justice roll down like waters and righteousness like a mighty stream." Somehow the preacher must say with Jesus, "The Spirit of the Lord is upon me, because He hath anointed me," and He's anointed me to deal with the problems of the poor.

Dr. King went on to talk about how he and five other pastors boarded a commercial flight from Atlanta to Memphis. The passengers had just settled in when the pilot said over the PA there would be a delay while the plane was inspected for bombs—a precaution because Dr. King was on the plane. When Dr. King reached Memphis, he was informed of still more threats against his life. He concluded:

> Well, I don't know what will happen now. We've got some difficult days ahead. But it really doesn't matter with me now, because I've been to the mountaintop. And I don't mind.

Like anybody, I would like to live a long life. Longevity has its place. But I'm not concerned about that now. I just want to do God's will. And He's allowed me to go up to the mountain. And I've looked over. And I've seen the Promised Land. I may not get there with you. But I want you to know tonight, that we, as a people, will get to the promised land!

And so I'm happy, tonight.
I'm not worried about anything.
I'm not fearing any man.
Mine eyes have seen the glory of the coming of the Lord.[7]

Dr. King had come to Memphis to support black sanitation workers who received less pay than white workers. He delivered this speech April 3, 1968, and it was the last speech he ever gave. The next evening, Dr. King stood on the balcony of the Lorraine Motel in Memphis, talking to friends about the planned meeting that night. An assassin fired a single bullet from a rooming house across the street, and Dr. King fell mortally wounded.

Like the prophet Amos, Dr. King thundered a vision of freedom and justice for all people—a vision he communicated with urgency and passion. Dr. King was only thirty-nine years old when he died, but he packed a lifetime of visionary leadership into that short span of time. His vision—his dream—was so powerful and compelling that our society continued moving toward his vision even after his death.

Keep communicating hope. Keep envisioning a better world. Let justice roll down like waters, and let righteousness flow like a mighty stream.

DANIEL: MAN OF VISION, INTERPRETER OF DREAMS

The Book of Daniel is full of dreams and visions, some frightening and some beautiful. It's an "apocalypse"—a revelation of things to come. Daniel was a learned young Jewish man who was led captive from his homeland and exiled in Babylon, along with thousands of Jews from the southern kingdom of Judah. The Babylonian exile began around 597 B.C., almost 170 years after the Assyrian conquest of the northern kingdom.

There are two major sections in Daniel—Daniel 1-6, six narratives about Daniel and his fellow captives in the court of Babylonian king Nebuchadnezzar and Persian king Cyrus; and Daniel 7-12, containing four visions of future events. One of the most significant of these visions takes place in Daniel 9, in which Daniel fasts and prays, pleading for God to return His people home to Jerusalem. In response to Daniel's prayer, the angel Gabriel comes to Daniel and says:

Daniel, I have now come to give you insight and understanding. As soon as you began to pray, a word went out, which I have come to tell you, for you are highly esteemed. Therefore, consider the word and understand the vision:

Seventy "sevens" are decreed for your people and your holy city to finish transgression, to put an end to sin, to atone for wickedness, to bring in everlasting righteousness, to seal up vision and prophecy and to anoint the Most Holy Place.

Know and understand this: From the time the word goes out to restore and rebuild Jerusalem until the Anointed One, the ruler, comes, there will be seven "sevens," and sixty-two "sevens." It will be rebuilt with streets and a trench, but in times of trouble. After the sixty-two "sevens," the Anointed One will be put to death and will have nothing. The people of the ruler who will come will destroy the city and the sanctuary. The end will come like a flood: War will continue until the end, and desolations have been decreed. He will confirm a covenant with many for one "seven." In the middle of the "seven" he will put an end to sacrifice and offering. And at the temple he will set up an abomination that causes desolation, until the end that is decreed is poured out on him. (Dan. 9:22b-27 NIV)

For centuries, this prophetic vision mystified scholars of the Jewish and Christian faiths. Then, in the 1890s, Sir Robert Anderson, a high-ranking police commissioner at Scotland Yard, wrote a book called *The Coming Prince*. In that book, Anderson worked out the meaning of this prophecy with mathematical precision. He realized that the seven "sevens" of years plus the sixty-two "sevens" of years that the angel Gabriel spoke of equaled sixty-nine "sevens" of years. Sixty-nine times seven equals 483.

Anderson also noticed this key phrase: "from the time the word goes out to restore and rebuild Jerusalem." In a flash of insight, he realized that this phrase referred to the decree of King Artaxerxes I of Persia—the pagan ruler who ordered the rebuilding of Jerusalem. Consulting the historical Book of Nehemiah and evidence from secular historians, Anderson determined that the decree to rebuild Jerusalem had to have been issued on March 14, 445 B.C. So this prophecy of Daniel predicted that, from March 14, 445 B.C. until "the Anointed One," the Messiah, would officially arrive as Israel's King, would be a span of 483 years.

The ancient Jews and Babylonians used a 360-day calendar, not the 365-day calendar we use today. So Anderson multiplied 360 days by 483 years to get a total of 173,880 days. Then he counted the number of days from the decree of Artaxerxes to rebuild Jerusalem. He arrived at a date of Sunday, April 6, A.D. 32. This is believed to be Palm Sunday, the day Jesus of Nazareth entered the city of Jerusalem and was hailed as the King of the Jews.

The prophecy of Gabriel in Daniel 9 predicted *the exact date* of Jesus's triumphant entry into Jerusalem as Israel's King. This is amazing enough—but even more amazing is the fact that the proof of Daniel's fulfilled prophecy was right there in the Old Testament, hiding in plain sight, for century after century until Sir Robert Anderson did the math in the 1890s.

Gabriel also told Daniel: "After the sixty-two 'sevens,' the Anointed One will be put to death and will have nothing." Less than a week after the Lord's triumphal entry into Jerusalem on Palm Sunday, Jesus was arrested, tried, and put to death on the cross. The vision that Daniel receives is incredibly detailed and accurate.

But there's still *more* prophetic insight in Daniel's vision, because Gabriel then says, "The people of the ruler who will come will destroy the city and the sanctuary." Who is "the ruler who will come" nearly five centuries after this vision takes place? This ruler is a Roman general named Titus. In A.D. 70, the Roman army under Titus will lay siege to Jerusalem and destroy the Temple. Titus will later become Emperor of Rome. Yet, at the time Daniel received this vision, the Roman empire didn't exist. At that time, Rome was little more than a smallish town perched on the Palatine Hill.

Yet everything the angel told Daniel was fulfilled, exactly in the timeframe the angel described. And there's still more to this prophecy, including a seven-year period that Bible scholars believe still lies in our future. It's a seven-year series of events known as the Great Tribulation. You will find this same seven-year period described by Jesus in

Matthew 24 and by John in Revelation 11. The prophecies of Daniel, Jesus, and Revelation are amazingly consistent.

So who was the prophet Daniel?

After being exiled to Babylon, Daniel served in the royal court of King Nebuchadnezzar. Later, after the Babylonian kingdom was conquered by Persia, Daniel served in the royal court King Cyrus in the Persian capital of Susa. Daniel probably experienced his last recorded vision at the age of eighty-five.

Daniel's name means "God is My Judge." The theme of Daniel is that the God who saved Daniel and his friends from their enemies will be faithful to save His people. This doesn't mean we will never face obstacles, opposition, or danger. It simply means that no matter what happens to us, even if we are shoved into a fiery furnace or a den of lions, God will be our defender.

After being led as captives into Babylon, Daniel and his three friends, Hananiah, Mishael, and Azariah, were made to serve in the court of King Nebuchadnezzar. The Babylonians gave Daniel the name Belteshazzar, and his friends were renamed Shadrach, Meshach, and Abednego. Despite their youth, Daniel and his friends possessed a deep, godly wisdom that astonished the Babylonians.

One night, King Nebuchadnezzar dreamed of a giant statue made of four metals, with feet formed of mingled iron and clay. A stone fell from heaven and smashed the statute. The king awoke deeply troubled, and only Daniel could interpret the dream. He told the king the statue represented four kingdoms, beginning with Babylon. Ultimately, God would destroy all four kingdoms and replace them with a heavenly kingdom (Dan. 2 NIV).

In Daniel 4, King Nebuchadnezzar had another dream, in which a tree stood tall and strong, then was broken and thrown down, leaving a stump bound with bands of iron and bronze. Daniel was anguished when Nebuchadnezzar told him the dream.

"Your Majesty," Daniel said, "you are that tree!... You will be driven away from people and will live with the wild animals.... Your kingdom will be restored to you when you acknowledge that Heaven rules. Therefore, Your Majesty, be pleased to accept my advice: Renounce your sins by doing what is right, and your wickedness by being kind to the oppressed. It may be that then your prosperity will continue" (Dan. 4:22,25-27 NIV).

Nebuchadnezzar failed to take Daniel's advice. One day, the king was admiring himself for building Babylon "by my mighty power and for the glory of my majesty." The instant Nebuchadnezzar voiced this arrogant thought, God struck him with madness and took away his kingdom, just as Daniel had prophesied. Nebuchadnezzar remained insane for years. When he came to his senses, he praised God—and God restored his kingdom.

After Nebuchadnezzar died, his wicked son Belshazzar was king. Belshazzar hosted a grand feast, and he and his guests swilled wine from the ceremonial cups stolen from the Temple in Jerusalem. That evening, a disembodied hand appeared out of nowhere and wrote a mysterious message on the wall—*mene, mene, tekel, parsin*. Only Daniel could interpret the message: God had numbered the days of Belshazzar's evil reign, and his kingdom would be conquered by the Medes and Persians. Belshazzar tried to placate God by clothing Daniel in royal robes and promoting him to third-highest ruler in the kingdom—but God's judgment was final. That night, the Medes and Persians conquered Babylon and killed Belshazzar (Dan. 5 NIV).

The new king, Darius the Mede, made Daniel chief advisor. Daniel's jealous rivals tricked the king into issuing a decree that anyone who prays to anyone other than Darius should be executed.

Darius didn't realize that Daniel would never go along with such a decree. Daniel not only disobeyed the decree, but he made a public spectacle of praying to God at his window so that the whole city would see.

Darius was forced to carry out the punishment he had decreed, and Daniel was cast into the lions' den. God protected Daniel from the lions—and as a result, Darius sent Daniel's accusers to the lions' den. Then he restored Daniel to his leadership position (Dan. 6 NIV).

In Daniel chapters 7 through 11, Daniel sees a series of visions of future events. These visions conclude on a note of triumph: God's faithful people will be preserved and God will establish His Kingdom on the Earth.

What are the leadership lessons we can learn from the prophet Daniel?

FIRST LESSON: *Leaders of vision are people of conviction and courage.*

Daniel was a man of extraordinary vision, a man who received amazing insights and wisdom directly from God. Because he lived in such intimate fellowship with God, Daniel had an unshakable confidence in God's provision and protection. Daniel and his three friends trusted God so completely that they could stand before kings and say, "God can deliver us from your hand. And even if He chooses not to deliver us, even if we die in the furnace or the jaws of the lions, we will worship only God."

They had courage and boldness in the face of a gruesome death because they had confidence in God.

SECOND LESSON: *Leaders of vision do not compromise their beliefs and principles.*

Our vision must be built on our beliefs and principles. We cannot abandon our principles without undermining our vision—so our leadership vision protects us against compromise and defection.

When leaders get mired in scandal, when corporations are rocked by corruption, when churches are torn by division, when nations experience spiraling debt and social chaos, it's often because there's no vision to bind people together around common beliefs. Daniel and his companions never strayed from their faith in God. When Daniel's enemies tried to destroy him, they could find no wrongdoing to charge him with. They were forced to use Daniel's integrity against him—and the effort backfired.

Cling to your principles, your faith, and your vision. Make sure that the worst thing your enemies can say about you is that you have absolute faith and integrity.

Daniel 6:1 tells us that King Darius appointed 120 minor governors, and placed three executive vice presidents over them to keep them honest. Daniel was one of those executive vice presidents. Darius knew that Daniel was a principled leader, a man of integrity who could always be trusted. Daniel's moral vision was crystal clear because it was built on a foundation of faith and principles.

THIRD LESSON: *Leaders of vision stand apart.*

The magicians and wise men of Babylon were unable to interpret Nebuchadnezzar's dreams. Only Daniel could interpret them. The wise men of Babylon could not interpret the handwriting on the wall. Only Daniel could interpret it. The wise men of Babylon plotted against Daniel and tried to destroy him, but they ended up destroying themselves.

If you are a person of vision, if you can interpret events, trends, and challenges to the organization, if you can spot trouble on the horizon and solve problems before they become crises, if you can successfully navigate the turbulent waters of change, then you will stand apart from the vast majority of people in your organization. Vision is a rare trait. Those who possess it stand apart from everyone else. Daniel was a leader of vision, and this trait made him indispensable to kings.

FOURTH LESSON: *Leaders of vision will face opposition.*
As you achieve your visionary goals, rivals will try to take you down. Have you ever seen a bucket of live crabs at a seafood market? They scrabble over each other, and if one starts to climb out of the bucket, the others will pull him back down. If crabs could ever get their act together and help each other, they could escape from the bucket. But crab nature will never change—and neither will human nature.

As a leader of vision, you will distinguish yourself and be noticed. You'll have opportunities for promotion. That's when the opposition will begin. Crabby people will try to pull you down. Don't focus your energy on your rivals. Instead, stay focused on your vision and goals.

Daniel never accused his enemies or defended himself. He focused on his vision, he kept serving his king, he kept praying to God—and the enemies who attacked him ultimately did themselves in.

FIFTH LESSON: *Leaders of vision face the hard truths and deliver bad news when necessary.*
It doesn't take courage or vision to be a yes-man. But it took real courage for Daniel to speak the truth to the three kings he served— Nebuchadnezzar, Belshazzar, and Darius the Mede. These kings could have had him killed for delivering bad news from God. Daniel told the truth anyway.

There's no guarantee that delivering bad news will get you promoted. It might get you fired. Tell the truth anyway. Don't flatter higher-ups and tell them only what they want to hear. If they are competent leaders, they'll reward you for speaking the truth. Bosses who "shoot the messenger" and shut their ears to the truth seldom last long.

SIXTH LESSON: *Righteous visionaries trust in God.*

Daniel 6:23 tells us that when Daniel was released from the lions' den, "no wound was found on him, because he had trusted in his God." I want to be known as a visionary leader who always trusts in God. He will shield us from scheming rivals, fiery furnaces, and hungry lions. He will lead us over the obstacles we face every day. No wound will be found on us if we trust in Him.

Samuel, Amos, and Daniel were three leaders who saw the future because God gave them visions. You and I may not have the supernatural pipeline to heaven they had, but we serve the same God they served. He still gives us the ability to see ahead, picture the possibilities, set the goals, and determine the processes to reach those goals. He gives us the inspiration and motivation to shape a better future for His glory.

Leaders of vision look beyond the present crisis, and glimpse the infinite vista of God's eternal plan. Leaders of vision paint word pictures that energize and motivate their followers. Leaders of vision call their followers to a deeper faith, a stronger commitment, a higher purpose.

Whether in the church, the business world, or in any other arena of leadership, visionary leaders make the future as tangible, vivid, and memorable as if it had already happened. To be a great leader, be a leader of vision.

CHAPTER 2: QUESTIONS FOR REFLECTION AND DISCUSSION

1. Should vision be the first and foundational side of the Seven Sides of Leadership? Or is one of the other sides more fundamental and essential? Explain your answer.

2. Are Samuel, Amos, and Daniel good role models of visionary leadership that we can learn from and follow? Why or why not?

3. In 1 Samuel 3:1, we read, "In those days the word of the Lord was rare; there were not many visions." In what ways are the times we live in today like the times in which Samuel lived?

   What lessons do you learn from Samuel that you can apply to your leadership arena?

4. Samuel learned at an early age to listen for the voice of the Lord. How can you apply this insight to your own life as a visionary leader? What steps can you take to be a better listener for God's voice?

5. Though Amos was an outsider, he was bold and fearless in announcing the vision God had given him. How can you apply the lessons of Amos's life to your own leadership challenges?

   Is Amos a visionary leader you can identify with? Why or why not?

6. Visionary leaders like Daniel inevitably face obstacles and opposition. What lessons can you learn from Daniel's life about dealing with opposition? How can you begin applying these lessons to your leadership life right now?

7. What role did prayer play in the visionary leadership of Daniel? What lessons about prayer can you learn from Daniel and apply to your own life?

PETER AND PAUL: LEADING BY COMMUNICATING

E veryone knows Dr. Martin Luther King's "I Have a Dream Speech," which he delivered from the steps of the Lincoln Memorial on Wednesday, August 28, 1963. But few know the role gospel singer Mahalia Jackson played in Dr. King's most famous speech.

Thanks to my mother, I was there on the National Mall that day. Mom was a great fan of Dr. King, so she arranged for my sister and me to be in our nation's capital for the March on Washington.

Dr. King had Mahalia Jackson perform just before he got up to speak. She sang "I Been 'Buked and I Been Scorned" in that slow, soaring contralto voice. The lyrics are powerful:

> I've been 'buked and I've been scorned
> Tryin' to make this journey all alone
> You may talk about me sure as you please
> Talk about me sure as you please
> Children, talk about me sure as you please
> Your talk will never drive me down to my knees
> Jesus died to set me free.

Then Dr. King got up to deliver the speech now known as "I Have a Dream." Earlier drafts of that speech had a less memorable title—"Normalcy, Never Again." The most famous lines of that speech—the rolling refrains of "I have a dream"—were not in his notes or on his mind as he began that speech.

Dr. King had given a speech with the "I have a dream" refrain two months earlier in Detroit. Mahalia Jackson had sung at that event, too. She remembered how Dr. King's dream had thrilled her soul. When Dr. King was about ten minutes into his prepared speech, Mahalia Jackson called out, "Tell 'em about the dream, Martin!"

King continued his prepared remarks for another sentence or two.

Mahalia called out again, "Tell 'em about the dream!"

And at that moment, Dr. King pushed his notes over to the left. He literally went off-script and ad-libbed the rest of the speech. "So even though we face the difficulties of today and tomorrow," he said, "I still have a dream."

If Mahalia Jackson had not spoken up, if she had not called out, "Tell 'em about the dream," that speech would have been a very different speech. If Dr. King had not told the crowd about his dream that day, how would history have changed? We'll never know. But I don't think the speech would have impacted history as it did if Dr. King hadn't told us about his dream. Dr. King communicated his vision to the world because Mahalia shouted, "Tell 'em about the dream!"

One of Mahalia Jackson's favorite gospel songs was "There is a Balm in Gilead." It contains these words of encouragement for leaders who feel inadequate as communicators:

If you can't preach like Peter,
If you can't pray like Paul,
Just tell the love of Jesus,
And say He died for all.

I love those words. They have a lot of meaning for me because I do a lot of public speaking. I can't preach like Peter and I can't pray like Paul, but I will gladly tell the love of Jesus, anytime, anyplace. Even though we may not be the communicators Peter and Paul were, these two leaders of the early church have a lot to teach us about being more effective communicators.

Let's look at Peter and Paul and see how they exemplified the Second Side of Leadership—Communication.

COMMUNICATING THE VISION

It's hard to imagine two unlikelier candidates for leadership in the early church than Peter and Paul. Peter was an uneducated Galilean fisherman. Jesus recruited him by the seashore and assigned him a leadership role. Paul was an enemy of Christ and a persecutor of the church—yet Jesus appeared to Paul and called him to become the greatest missionary of all time.

Peter and Paul were leaders of the newborn church, and they led by communicating. The first half of the Book of Acts deals largely with the leadership of Peter in the early church, beginning with his great Pentecost sermon in Acts 2. About halfway through the Book of Acts, the narrative shifts focus from the leadership of Peter to the leadership of Paul.

Both Peter and Paul were men of vision, and both received their vision for the church from Jesus Himself. Peter walked with Jesus and was mentored by Him almost from the beginning of the Lord's earthly ministry. And Paul dramatically encountered the risen Lord Jesus on the road to Damascus.

The First Side of Leadership is Vision—but what good is a vision from God if you can't communicate that vision to others? That's why the Second Side of Leadership, Communication, is equally important.

Dave Kraft served with The Navigators for thirty-seven years, and is now the discipleship pastor at Village Church in Irvine, California. In *Leaders Who Last*, he wrote:

> One of the primary roles of an effective leader for the twenty-first century is that of vision caster. This would include crafting and birthing a vision, then cultivating and clarifying the vision through creative communication. The leader doesn't do it alone, but should be the primary point person for this communication. I have yet to see any success when the leader delegates the responsibility for the caretaking of the vision to a board or committee. It is the leader's responsibility to ensure the vision is kept before the people.[8]

Leadership guru Tom Peters once observed:

> Leaders are people of action.... But leaders are also great talkers. Leadership takes an almost bottomless supply of verbal energy: working the phones, staying focused on your message, repeating the same mantra until you can't stand the sound of your own voice—and then repeating it some more, because just when you start to become bored witless with the message, it's probably starting to seep into the organization. You can't be a leader these days and be the strong, silent type. You have to be an endless talker, a tireless communicator.[9]

Some leaders make the mistake of thinking that "communicating the vision" means calling a meeting and saying it once. But most people don't grasp the vision in a single moment. They need to see it, hear it, and experience the vision again and again. Often, it is not until the tenth or twentieth repetition that the listener finally says, "Oh! Now I get it!"

Communication is repetition. Great leaders communicate the vision again and again.

HOW TO COMMUNICATE LIKE PETER

Peter was born Simon, son of Jonah. When he first encountered Jesus, he was a fisherman in the village of Bethsaida, near Capernaum. There's no direct mention of Peter's wife, but we know he was married because three of the four gospels tell us that Jesus healed Peter's mother-in-law in Capernaum.[10] Peter was one of the first disciples of Jesus called, and he was a brother of another disciple, Andrew.

A key turning point in Peter's life is found in Matthew 16:13-19. There Jesus asked the disciples, "Who do people say the Son of Man is?" After the disciples gave various answers, Jesus asked, "Who do *you* say I am?" Peter spoke up and said, "You are the Messiah, the Son of the living God."

"Blessed are you, Simon son of Jonah," Jesus said, "for this was not revealed to you by flesh and blood, but by my Father in heaven. And I tell you that you are Peter, and on this rock I will build my church, and the gates of Hades will not overcome it. I will give you the keys of the Kingdom of Heaven; whatever you bind on earth will be bound in heaven, and whatever you loose on earth will be loosed in heaven."

The name Peter, of course, means "rock." I believe that when Jesus gave Peter that name, He was communicating a vision to Peter—a vision of the rocklike, stable character Jesus saw in Peter's future, a stability that Simon, son of Jonah, had not yet demonstrated.

There are more layers of meaning to this passage. When Jesus gave Simon a new name, Peter the Rock, he also referred to Peter's confession that Jesus is the Messiah, the Son of the living God. This statement of faith is the cornerstone on which the Christian church stands. In Ephesians 2:20, Paul says the church is "built on the foundation of the apostles and prophets, with Christ Jesus himself as the chief cornerstone." And in 1 Peter 2:6, Peter himself writes (quoting Isaiah 28:16):

> For in Scripture it says:
> "See, I lay a stone in Zion,
>   a chosen and precious cornerstone,
> and the one who trusts in him
>   will never be put to shame."

All of church history proceeds from this one essential fact, that Jesus of Nazareth is the long-prophesied Messiah. The church exists, grows, and increases in influence whenever a believer makes this confession and witnesses to the same fact that Peter confessed: Jesus is the Messiah, the Son of the living God.

We in the Christian church are taking this message to a lost and dying world. We are assaulting the gates of hell, and those gates cannot withstand our attack, because Jesus is the Messiah, the Son of the living God. That is an amazing vision, and a powerful message to communicate. The first believer to communicate that message was Peter.

In the Gospels and the Book of Acts, Peter is always listed first among the apostles. He is also frequently the spokesman for the apostles. Paul called Peter one of the pillars of the early church (Gal. 2:9 NIV).

In Acts 2, on the Day of Pentecost, Peter was inspired by the Holy Spirit to deliver an impromptu sermon, without notes or preparation. The scene was an open-air marketplace in Jerusalem, and the centerpiece of Peter's message was Jesus Himself:

> Fellow Israelites, listen to this: Jesus of Nazareth was a man accredited by God to you by miracles, wonders and signs, which God did among you through him, as you yourselves know. This man was handed over to you by God's deliberate plan and foreknowledge; and you, with the help of wicked men, put him to death by nailing him to the cross. But God raised him from the dead, freeing him from the agony of death, because it was impossible for death to keep its hold on him....
>
> Therefore let all Israel be assured of this: God has made this Jesus, whom you crucified, both Lord and Messiah. (Acts 2:22-24, 36 NIV)

Peter used the words of the Old Testament prophets to prove that Jesus was, in fact, the Messiah. It was a good-news/bad-news message. The bad news was that the very people he was preaching to had crucified the Messiah. The good news was that God had raised Jesus from the dead. Peter's listeners were stricken with guilt and they asked Peter and the apostles, "Brothers, what shall we do?"

"Repent and be baptized," Peter said, "every one of you, in the name of Jesus Christ for the forgiveness of your sins." Those who received Peter's message were baptized immediately—and the church increased by 3,000 souls in a single day.

The rapid growth of the newborn church caught the attention of the Sanhedrin, the council of religious judges in Jerusalem. This was the same council that had plotted the death of Jesus. The members of the Sanhedrin thought they had stamped out this movement when they maneuvered the Roman officials into executing Jesus. Now the Christian movement was growing faster than ever—and this trouble-maker named Peter was the new head of the movement. Something had to be done about him.

In Acts 3, Peter and John were in the Temple courtyard, and they healed a lame man. This miracle of healing attracted a huge crowd, giving Peter the opportunity to communicate the gospel once again. As Peter preached, the religious leaders seized Peter and John, and hauled them off to jail. Though Peter hadn't finished his sermon, people responded and the number of believers swelled to 5,000 (Acts 4:4 NIV).

The following day, Peter and John were brought before the Sanhedrin and put on trial. The high priest and other judges questioned Peter and John about the miracle of healing: "By what power or what name did you do this?" Peter replied:

> Rulers and elders of the people! If we are being called to account today for an act of kindness shown to a man who was lame and are being asked how he was healed, then know this, you and all the people of Israel: It is by the name of Jesus Christ of Nazareth, whom you crucified but whom God raised from the dead, that this man stands before you healed. Jesus is
>
> > "the stone you builders rejected,
> > which has become the cornerstone."
>
> Salvation is found in no one else, for there is no other name under heaven given to mankind by which we must be saved. (Acts 4:8-12 NIV)

The leaders of the Sanhedrin were astonished at the words of Peter and John—and they realized these two men, both unschooled fishermen—had been transformed by their time with Jesus. The man God had healed through Peter and John stood in the courtroom as Exhibit A. The Sanhedrin faced a crisis. Somehow, these judges had to silence Peter and John, and stop this movement from growing. But they feared a backlash from Christians and Christian sympathizers.

The Sanhedrin decided to threaten Peter and John and command them not to speak about Jesus. The apostles answered, "Which is right in God's eyes: to listen to you, or to Him?… We cannot help speaking about what we have seen and heard."

The Sanhedrin threatened Peter and John one more time, then let them go. But the confrontation wasn't over.

Later, as Peter and the apostles were preaching and healing at the Temple, the high priest's guards arrested and jailed the apostles. During the night, an angel of the Lord released them from the jail and told them to continue preaching in the Temple courts. In the morning, when the high priest assembled the Sanhedrin to put the apostles on trial, the guards found the jail was empty.

Then a man arrived from the Temple with news that the apostles were back at work, preaching about Jesus. This time, the guards hesitated to physically seize the apostles for fear of the crowds. Instead, they pleaded with the apostles to stand before the Sanhedrin. The apostles agreed.

As the apostles went before the Sanhedrin, the high priest was furious. "You have filled Jerusalem with your teaching," he said, "and are determined to make us guilty of this man's blood."

"We must obey God rather than human beings," Peter replied. "The God of our ancestors raised Jesus from the dead—whom you killed by hanging him on a cross. God exalted him to his own right hand as Prince and Savior that he might bring Israel to repentance and forgive their sins. We are witnesses of these things, and so is the Holy Spirit, whom God has given to those who obey him."

Instead of backing off, Peter doubled down on his indictment of the Sanhedrin. Nothing infuriates evil people like the truth—and Peter just can't stop telling the truth!

The high priest and other members of the Sanhedrin shouted for Peter's death—but one member of the Sanhedrin, a scholar of religious law named Gamaliel, rose and spoke. He warned the Sanhedrin against harming the apostles. Other cults had arisen in the past, but after their leaders were killed, their followers scattered. Leave these Christians alone, and this cult will probably collapse as well. But if this message is from God, it would be foolish to fight against Him.

The Sanhedrin agreed, so the high priest had the apostles flogged and released. Peter and his friends walked away bleeding—but also rejoicing. They were happy that God had found them worthy to suffer persecution for the sake of Jesus. Ignoring the orders of the Sanhedrin, they continued preaching about Jesus.

What leadership lessons can we learn from Peter, one of the two great communicators of the early church?

FIRST LESSON: *Great communication starts with a great vision.* Peter referred to a vision of the glorification of Jesus in his sermon following the healing of the lame man: "The God of Abraham, Isaac and Jacob, the God of our fathers, has glorified his servant Jesus" (Acts 3:13 NIV). And in his second epistle, Peter again describes a vision of the majesty of Jesus:

> For we did not follow cleverly devised stories when we told you about the coming of our Lord Jesus Christ in power,

but we were eyewitnesses of his majesty. He received honor and glory from God the Father when the voice came to him from the Majestic Glory, saying, "This is my Son, whom I love; with him I am well pleased." We ourselves heard this voice that came from heaven when we were with him on the sacred mountain. (2 Pet. 1:16-18 NIV)

What does Peter mean when he says, "We were eyewitnesses of his majesty"? He is referring to an incident in Matthew 17, Mark 9, and Luke 9: the Transfiguration of Jesus. I believe the apostle John also referred to the Transfiguration when he wrote, "The Word became flesh and made his dwelling among us. We have seen his glory, the glory of the one and only Son, who came from the Father, full of grace and truth" (John 1:14 NIV).

Jesus took three of his closest apostles, Peter, James, and John, onto a mountain to pray. There, the three apostles saw the robes of Jesus shine with blinding white light. As they watched, two Old Testament heroes, Moses and Elijah, appeared next to Jesus and talked with Him.

All three apostles were terrified. Peter babbled to Jesus about building shelters for Him and Moses and Elijah. Then a cloud covered Jesus, Moses, and Elijah, and God's voice came from the cloud, saying, "This is my Son, whom I love. Listen to Him!"

This is the vision Peter witnessed. And when I say "vision," I don't mean it was all a dream. It happened literally, physically, and powerfully. The three apostles witnessed this scene with their own eyes—and they remembered the glory of the transfigured Christ for the rest of their lives.

What did the Transfiguration mean? God gave these three apostles a vision of things to come. God showed them how the glorified Lord Jesus would appear at His Second Coming. He first came to earth in lowliness and humility as a helpless baby, and he died the death of a criminal. When he returns, His true glory will shine for all to see. As the apostle John wrote in the Book of Revelation:

> Look, he is coming with the clouds, and every eye will see him, even those who pierced him; and all peoples on earth will mourn because of him. So shall it be! Amen. "I am the Alpha and the Omega," says the Lord God, who is, and who was, and who is to come, the Almighty. (Rev. 1:7-8 NIV)

And I think the Transfiguration had another purpose. God showed these apostles that Jesus was not a mere human teacher, not a political revolutionary, not a mere religious leader. The apostles needed to know that Jesus was even greater than Moses and Elijah. Jesus is the Son of the living God.

Moments after the Transfiguration began, it was over. The clouds dissipated, the clothes of Jesus no longer shone with light. Moses and Elijah had vanished. Jesus and the three apostles were alone on the mountainside. Jesus commanded them not to tell anyone what they had seen until after His resurrection. Peter, James, and John did as Jesus told them, keeping the matter to themselves.

That vision on the mountain was unforgettable. Peter's leadership career began with a vision of Jesus the Messiah. That vision motivated and emboldened him throughout his life. The memory of the blindingly radiant Lord Jesus probably sustained Peter in the last hours of his life, as he was crucified upside-down in Rome. Leadership starts with a vision.

SECOND LESSON: *Great communicators seek the filling of the Holy Spirit.*

In Peter's great Pentecost sermon, God gave those first believers the gift of His Spirit. The Spirit gave the apostles spiritual gifts—supernatural abilities—that enabled them to carry out their roles in the early church with amazing effectiveness.

In Acts 4:8, where Peter speaks before the assembled Sanhedrin, we read, "Then Peter, filled with the Holy Spirit, said to them." Peter had learned the lessons of past failures. He had learned the danger of trying to do anything in his own strength. He knew he needed the power of the Holy Spirit.

The filling of the Holy Spirit begins with honest, searching prayer. We ask God to remove any sin or selfishness that would hinder His complete control of our thoughts and words. We ask Him to cleanse us, to renew our minds, to make us sensitive to His leading. We ask His Spirit to fill us and control us.

Before the Holy Spirit came into Peter's life, he was an impetuous failure who had denied his Lord three times. After the Holy Spirit fell upon Peter, he was transformed into a man of unfathomable wisdom, unbreakable faith, unbending integrity, and unshakable courage. What a transformation!

This same Holy Spirit is available to you and me, in the same way, in the same measure. Just as Peter was filled with the Holy Spirit when he got up to speak, you and I can be filled with the Spirit. We can receive supernatural power, encouragement, and guidance whenever we speak. To communicate like Peter, be filled with the Spirit.

THIRD LESSON: *Godly communicators are always ready to speak God's truth.*

In 1 Peter 3:15, the apostle Peter tells us to always be prepared to speak: "But in your hearts revere Christ as Lord. Always be prepared to give an answer to everyone who asks you to give the reason for the hope that you have. But do this with gentleness and respect."

Preparation begins with our attitude toward the Lord Jesus Christ. "In your hearts," Peter says, "revere Christ as Lord." This is a crucial statement. Peter is telling us that, in every communication opportunity, start with submission to the lordship of Jesus Christ. He is Lord, we are not. When we speak, our goal should be to obey him, serve him, and glorify him—not to serve and glorify ourselves.

Next, we should prepare what we will say. Yes, Peter spoke extemporaneously, letting the wisdom of the Holy Spirit pour through him as he addressed the eager crowds or the hostile Sanhedrin. But this same Peter encourages us to think through our answers to the questions unbelievers toss at us. We should know what we believe and why we believe it. Then we will never be caught off-guard by an opportunity to share Christ.

The better prepared we are, the more confident we will be. To communicate like Peter, prepare your heart by submitting to the Lord, prepare your mind by planning your message, and prepare your spirit through the filling of the Holy Spirit. Next, let's look at the leadership example of Paul.

HOW TO COMMUNICATE LIKE PAUL

In the Scriptures, an apostle is a person who has been commissioned (that is, given a mission) by Jesus Himself. After Judas Iscariot betrayed Jesus and committed suicide, the early church needed to appoint a new apostle. Peter laid out the conditions for being an apostle: the new twelfth apostle had to be someone who had been with Jesus throughout His earthly ministry. The church chose a believer named Matthias to be the twelfth apostle.

Then came Paul. He had a miraculous encounter with Jesus on the road to Damascus. Jesus asked Paul, "Why do you persecute Me?" That encounter brought Paul to his knees. After his conversion, Paul spent time in the Arabian desert (Gal. 1:17 NIV), where he encountered Christ again, possibly through visions. As Paul wrote to the Galatians, "I want you to know, brothers and sisters, that the gospel I preached is not of human origin. I did not receive it from any man, nor was I taught it; rather, I received it by revelation from Jesus Christ" (Gal. 1:11-12 NIV).

So Paul became the thirteenth apostle. Though Paul was not one of the original Twelve, and had never met Jesus during His earthly ministry, the early church accepted Paul as a true apostle. Like the Twelve, Paul had been commissioned by Jesus Himself—though not at the same time and not in the same way as the Twelve.

Paul became the first great missionary of the church. He founded churches throughout Asia Minor (now known as Turkey) and in Europe. He was a Jewish scholar, a member of the Pharisee sect, before his conversion to Christianity. He was also a Roman citizen by birth. As a result, he was comfortable moving and speaking in either the Jewish world or the Gentile world of the Roman Empire.

Paul used his dual citizenship to his advantage in every communication opportunity. Among Jews, he spoke the Hebrew language, practiced Jewish culture and traditions, and understood the Jewish religion inside and out. Among the Greeks and Romans, he could relate to their culture, philosophy, and religious ideas.

Let's focus on one event during Paul's second missionary journey, a sermon he delivered on Mars Hill (also called Areopagus) in Athens, Greece. We find this speech in Acts 17. Prior to arriving in Athens, Paul has preached in two Greek cities, Thessalonica and Berea. Paul narrowly escaped from a blood-thirsty mob in Thessalonica, but the Bereans welcomed his message. Soon, however, Paul's enemies from Thessalonica caught up with him in Berea and stirred up the crowds against him.

Paul then went to Athens, a cosmopolitan crossroads of ideas and cultures. Because Athens welcomed new ideas, it was a much safer place for Paul to rest and plan his next move. As he entered the city and looked around, Paul saw that Athens was filled with idols to pagan gods. Paul's soul was oppressed by the proliferation of idols.

In Athens, as in every city Paul visited, he went first to the synagogue and preached Christ to the Jews in that city. He preached from the prophetic passages of the Hebrew Scriptures, showing that Jesus was the promised Messiah and the Savior of the human race.

Next, Paul took his message to the Agora (the marketplace) of Athens and preached Christ there. Paul's message attracted the attention of some of the philosophers of Athens, and they took him to a meeting of Greek intellectuals at Mars Hill—a site of Greek temples, cultural buildings, and the highest court of Athens. It was the Internet of ancient Greece, the place where people gathered to exchange news, gossip, and ideas.

The Athenians were fascinated to hear about other religions, so they invited Paul to speak. Luke, the author of Acts, tells us what happened next:

> Paul then stood up in the meeting of the Areopagus and said: "People of Athens! I see that in every way you are very religious. For as I walked around and looked carefully at your objects of worship, I even found an altar with this inscription: TO AN UNKNOWN GOD. So you are ignorant of the very thing you worship—and this is what I am going to proclaim to you.
>
> "The God who made the world and everything in it is the Lord of heaven and earth and does not live in temples built by human hands. And he is not served by human hands,

as if he needed anything. Rather, he himself gives everyone life and breath and everything else. From one man he made all the nations, that they should inhabit the whole earth; and he marked out their appointed times in history and the boundaries of their lands. God did this so that they would seek him and perhaps reach out for him and find him, though he is not far from any one of us. 'For in him we live and move and have our being.' As some of your own poets have said, 'We are his offspring.'

"Therefore since we are God's offspring, we should not think that the divine being is like gold or silver or stone— an image made by human design and skill. In the past God overlooked such ignorance, but now he commands all people everywhere to repent. For he has set a day when he will judge the world with justice by the man he has appointed. He has given proof of this to everyone by raising him from the dead." (Acts 17:22-31 NIV)

When the scholars and philosophers heard Paul preach about the resurrection of the dead, many openly jeered. But others said, "We want to hear you tell us more about the resurrection." Some became followers of Christ that day.

Paul's message on Mars Hill is a case study in leadership communication. Let's look at the communication lessons we can learn from Paul's Mars Hill speech.

FIRST LESSON: *Great communicators know their audience.*

When Paul arrived in Athens, he walked around the city, looking at idols of gold, silver, and stone. Paul tells us he "looked carefully" at the objects of worship in the city. He undoubtedly overheard conversations in the marketplace. He listened to what people were saying about their hopes, their fears, their problems. He knew there was no hope to be found in worshiping an idol made of metal or stone.

After studying his audience, he considered how best to communicate the good news of Jesus to people who had no background in the Hebrew Scriptures. With Jewish audiences, he cited the prophecies of Jesus from Genesis to Malachi. He could recite the messianic prophecies in the Psalms. He could talk about Jesus, the Suffering Servant from Isaiah 52—and on and on. But the Greeks had no background in the Hebrew Scriptures. To reach this audience, he had to invent a new and creative approach.

Once Paul had gauged his audience, he was careful to match his message to their needs and their culture. As he wrote to the believers in Corinth:

> Though I am free and belong to no one, I have made myself
> a slave to everyone, to win as many as possible. To the Jews
> I became like a Jew, to win the Jews. To those under the law
> I became like one under the law (though I myself am not
> under the law), so as to win those under the law. To those
> not having the law I became like one not having the law
> (though I am not free from God's law but am under Christ's
> law), so as to win those not having the law. To the weak I
> became weak, to win the weak. I have become all things to
> all people so that by all possible means I might save some. I
> do all this for the sake of the gospel, that I may share in its
> blessings. (1 Cor. 9:19-23 NIV)

As leaders, let's take the time to understand our audience—then let's communicate with them in a way that suits their unique needs.

SECOND LESSON: *Great communicators demonstrate empathy with their audience.*

Again and again, Paul makes a connection with his Greek listeners. He doesn't talk down to them—he talks straight across to them. He doesn't condemn them—he identifies with them. He doesn't berate them for being pagans and idolaters. He affirms them for being "very religious." He observes that they had built an altar to an "unknown god." He says, "you are ignorant of the very thing you worship," and he doesn't use "ignorant" as an insult. The Greeks themselves confess that there is a god who is unknown to them—a god they are ignorant of.

Paul uses their own altar to the "unknown god" as a touchstone, enabling him to talk about God in terms the Athenians can understand. "You are ignorant of the very thing you worship," Paul tells them, "and this is what I am going to proclaim to you." He built rapport by finding common ground with his audience.

Next, Paul started at Genesis and told the Athenians about the God who made the world, who doesn't live in temples, but gives life and breath to everything that lives. He made the nations, and He is not far from us. Then Paul quoted their favorite philosophers. He said, "For in him we live and move and have our being," citing a line by Epimenides of Knossos, a philosopher of the seventh century BC, from his poem *Cretica*. In the same verse, he says, "As some of your own poets have said, 'We are his offspring,'" citing a line from the poem *Phenomena* by the Stoic philosopher Aratus.

By quoting Greek philosophers to these philosophical Greeks, he translated the Christian gospel into cultural terms they could understand. To evangelize people, we need to empathize with them. People are much more willing to listen to our message when they know we understand them.

THIRD LESSON: *Great communicators reason calmly and persuasively—they don't browbeat their listeners into submission.*

When Paul came to a city, he always went first to the synagogue, where he would reason with his Jewish brothers from the Hebrew Scriptures. And in Athens, he reasoned with the Greeks from their own religious inscriptions and their own philosophers. He was intellectually and spiritually prepared to reason with anyone, at any time, about the good news of Jesus Christ.

The Athenian audience treated Paul and his message with respect. Some scoffed in disbelief when he talked of the resurrection, but others thought his message was intriguing and they wanted to hear more. Some believed in Christ that very day. Paul treated his listeners with respect, and they responded with respect. Acts 17:17 tells us, "So he reasoned in the synagogue with both Jews and God-fearing Greeks, as well as in the marketplace day by day with those who happened to be there." Reason and respect are key ingredients of effective communication.

Paul wrote in his letter to the church at Colossae, "Let your conversation be always full of grace, seasoned with salt, so that you may know how to answer everyone" (Col. 4:6 NIV). Conversation that is full of grace is kind, not combative; understanding, not overbearing; respectful, not reproachful. Conversation that is seasoned with salt is tasteful; it leaves a pleasant aftertaste. The speech of Christians should taste different from the bland, unsalted speech of the world.

Salt was also a preservative in the time of Paul, so conversation that is seasoned with salt preserves a spirit of cordiality between people. It prevents the conversation from being spoiled by conflict. Also, salt was a valuable commodity in Paul's day. It was even used like money as a medium of exchange. There's great value in speech that is seasoned with salt. If you communicate graciously and respectfully, seasoning your words to make them pleasant to the taste, you'll communicate effectively and persuasively, as Paul did.

FOURTH LESSON: *Great communicators are great listeners.*

Luke tells us that Paul "reasoned" in the synagogue and in the marketplace. This tells us that Paul didn't just preach—he had two-way conversations. He listened, he took questions, he answered objections, and he did so in a reasonable and respectful way. Paul was a great communicator because he was a great listener.

Authentic communication is a two-way street. Even if you are giving a speech before an audience, you should make eye contact with your listeners to make sure they're tracking with you. Gauge their mood and attentiveness, and adjust your speech to the cues you receive. If you see people fighting to stay awake, pump more energy into your voice and say, "Let me tell you a story." Audiences always sit up straight and pay attention when they know a story's coming.

Instead of lecturing people, reason with them. Stop now and then to invite questions or discussion. Have a conversation with your audience. Look for ways to turn a canned presentation into a genuine conversation.

FIFTH LESSON: *Great communicators love their listeners.*

In 1 Corinthians 13:1, Paul tells us that communication is meaningless without love. He wrote, "If I speak in the tongues of men or of angels, but do not have love, I am only a resounding gong or a clanging cymbal."

What kind of "love" is Paul talking about? He's not referring to affectionate or romantic feelings. He's saying we should care deeply and genuinely about what is best for our listeners. We should never stand before an audience and think, "How can I manipulate these people into giving me what I want? How can I convince them to support me? How can I get them to put money in my pocket?" Whenever we communicate, we should always think of what our audience needs. We should try to add value to their lives. If they sense our genuine love for them, they will trust us and follow us in return.

Paul goes on to describe the kind of love we should have as leaders and communicators: "Love is patient, love is kind. It does not envy, it does not boast, it is not proud. It does not dishonor others, it is not self-seeking, it is not easily angered, it keeps no record of wrongs. Love does not delight in evil but rejoices with the truth. It always protects, always trusts, always hopes, always perseveres." (1 Cor. 13:4-7 NIV)

The ability to stand in front of an audience and give a speech is a skill. Most people can learn it. But loving people the way Paul describes is a commitment. A leader who communicates authentic love for his listeners, who truly cares about their problems and needs, has the makings of a great leader.

That was the kind of leader Jesus was in His earthly ministry. Matthew 9:36 tells us that when Jesus saw the crowds, "He had compassion on them, because they were harassed and helpless, like sheep without a shepherd." Don't be a resounding gong or a clanging cymbal. Lead with love. Be a leader who can preach like Peter and pray like Paul.

While I was general manager of the Philadelphia 76ers, I got to know Phillies third baseman Mike Schmidt. My third son, Mike, is named after Mike Schmidt. I once heard Mike describe his philosophy of teamwork, which he distilled into a simple phrase, "Share the love." He explained, "Love is the most powerful motivator there is. I'm not talking about love as an emotion, but love as an unconditional commitment to each other on the team. When a team develops that indefinable quality called 'chemistry,' it's because love is in the air. Players feel liberated to take risks and achieve great things because they know their teammates will support them and uphold them whether the ball bounces their way or not. They know their teammates are pulling for them no matter what, because the team is built on a foundation of love."

The late UCLA basketball coach John Wooden communicated love to his players. Swen Nater played for Coach Wooden in the early 1970s, and he told me that Coach Wooden once said to his former players, "I didn't like you all the same, but I tried to love you all the same." The love Coach Wooden spoke of was the same kind of love the apostle Paul wrote about—love that is based on a commitment, not an emotion. It's a love that is patient, kind, humble, truthful, protective, trusting, and hopeful—a love that never fails.

The Second Side of Leadership is communication. And when great leaders communicate, the most important thing they communicate is love.

CHAPTER 3: QUESTIONS FOR REFLECTION AND DISCUSSION

1. The author suggests that it is impossible to lead effectively if you cannot communicate effectively. Agree or disagree?

   Can you name a great leader who was *not* an effective communicator? If you can name such a leader, what makes him or her an exception to the rule?

2. Do your communication skills enhance your leadership ability, or do they hinder your leadership ability?

   On a scale of 1 to 10, with 1 being very poor and 10 being excellent, how would you rate yourself as a communicator?

   Where do your communication skills need improvement?

3. Read Peter's Pentecost sermon in Acts 2, which he delivered passionately, impromptu and without notes. Where do you think Peter's ability to deliver such a speech came from?

   What would you need to do, what skills would you need to acquire, what resources would you need to tap into, to preach like Peter?

4. Peter said, "Always be prepared to give an answer to everyone who asks you to give the reason for the hope that you have." Do you feel prepared to share Christ with others at a moment's notice? If not, why not? What steps do you need to take this week to prepare yourself for the next opportunity to share your hope with others?

5. How did Paul demonstrate empathy with his audience in his Mars Hill speech? What steps can you take to demonstrate empathy with your listeners, in both your public speaking and one-on-one conversations?

6. Great communicators are great listeners. On a scale of 1 to 10, how would you rate yourself as a listener? What steps can you take to become a better listener?

7. Great communicators love their listeners. What steps can you take, as a speaker and leader, to show your audience you care and you love them with a Christlike love?

CHAPTER 4

NEHEMIAH: A LEADER WITH PEOPLE SKILLS

John Friel is the director of Blue Water Growth, a global consulting group specializing in transpacific business ventures. He once said, "I don't make anything. I don't design anything. I don't sell anything, so the real work of this company is all done by other people. My job is to create the environment for those people to be successful, and I believe if I'm out and get a feel for what the real workers are doing, then I think it enables me to do a better job of creating the environment for them."[11]

People who achieve great things through other people are called leaders. A leader can't do it all, but must rely on followers to achieve results. A coach relies on players to get the ball through the hoop or into the end zone. A CEO relies on managers and employees to make the company profitable. A pastor relies on elders and church members to carry out ministry goals. A general relies on officers and enlisted personnel to execute the battle plan.

The leader's job is to create an environment for followers and workers to be successful. It must be an environment of inspiration, motivation, affirmation, and cooperation. To create that kind of environment, a leader must possess abilities called people skills. That's why the Third Side of Leadership is people skills.

I define people skills as the ability to understand the people you lead, to empathize with them, and to build constructive relationships with them. People skills are nothing more or less than the social skills that enable you to get along with people, to resolve conflict with people, to negotiate with people, and to maintain mutually beneficial relationships with people. These seem like basic, easy-to-acquire skills—yet it's amazing how many people in leadership positions lack these essential skills.

A smile or a word of praise can energize your people for an entire week. Calling people by name is music to their ears. Demonstrating a personal interest in your people—acknowledging an employment anniversary or a birthday—can give a huge lift to someone on your team. A leader with good people skills will be slow to criticize, quick to praise, and eager to help.

President Dwight Eisenhower once said, "Leadership is the art of getting someone else to do something you want done because he wants to do it."[12] If that is true, then people skills are essential to leadership. In fact, people skills are one of the key factors that separate a genuine leader from a boss.

Bosses intimidate; leaders motivate. Bosses demand obedience; leaders inspire loyalty. Bosses assert power over others; leaders empower others. Bosses condemn mistakes; leaders praise good effort and encourage people to learn from mistakes. A boss without people skills takes credit for what others achieve. A leader with people skills says, "Look at what we accomplished together!"

One of the great biblical examples of the Third Side of Leadership is an Old Testament leader named Nehemiah.

PEOPLE SKILLS AND THE KING OF PERSIA

About six centuries before Christ, Nebuchadnezzar, king of Babylon, laid siege to Jerusalem, the capital of the southern kingdom of Judah. The Babylonians ultimately captured Jerusalem, destroyed the temple of Solomon, and led the Jewish people into exile. These events had been predicted by the prophet Jeremiah—but Jeremiah had also foretold an end to captivity after seventy years of exile in Babylon. Inspired by the Holy Spirit, Jeremiah wrote:

> This is what the Lord says: "When seventy years are completed for Babylon, I will come to you and fulfill my good promise to bring you back to this place. For I know the plans I have for you," declares the Lord, "plans to prosper you and not to harm you, plans to give you hope and a future. Then you will call on me and come and pray to me, and I will listen to you. You will seek me and find me when you seek me with all your heart. I will be found by you," declares the Lord, "and will bring you back from captivity. I will gather you from all the nations and places where I have banished you," declares the Lord, "and will bring you back to the place from which I carried you into exile." (Jer. 29:10-14 NIV)

The Persian Empire conquered Babylon in 539 BC, and the Persians allowed the Jews to return to their homeland. The people of Judah returned to find their once-glorious capital city in ruins. The walls and Temple of Jerusalem were reduced to rubble. The people who had remained in the land were economically, culturally, and spiritually devastated. Two leaders, Nehemiah and Ezra, worked together to rebuild and restore the city of Jerusalem and its people. Ezra was the leader of the spiritual reconstruction of the people; Nehemiah led the physical reconstruction of the city and the Temple.

The Book of Nehemiah opens after the Jewish exiles have begun returning to their homeland. Nehemiah was a Jewish official in the government of Persia. He lived in the capital city of Susa. One day, he received news from Jerusalem: "Those who survived the exile and are back in the province are in great trouble and disgrace. The wall of Jerusalem is broken down, and its gates have been burned with fire" (Neh. 1:1-3 NIV).

Nehemiah's response was emotional and prayerful. Nehemiah wrote, "When I heard these things, I sat down and wept. For some days I mourned and fasted and prayed before the God of heaven" (Neh. 1:4 NIV). The tragic state of his people and his homeland caused him to grieve and weep. Nehemiah poured out his anguish to God in prayer—and God heard his prayer.

We find Nehemiah's prayer in verses 5 through 10. There, Nehemiah acknowledged the greatness and love of God, confessed his own sins and the sins of his people, and remembered God's promise of forgiveness and restoration. Finally, Nehemiah asked God to move the heart of the Persian king, so that he would allow Nehemiah to go home to Jerusalem and rebuild the city.

Nehemiah was the cupbearer to the king. This is an important position of trust in the kingdom. Ancient kings worried continuously about assassination plots, and they needed to be able to trust the wine and the cupbearer who served it. Nehemiah had earned the king's trust. But Nehemiah was about to ask the Persian king for a huge favor, so he needed God's help in making the heart of the king receptive to his request.

Sometime later, in Nehemiah 2, Nehemiah was serving wine and the king noticed the sad demeanor of his cupbearer. The king asked why his cupbearer seemed unhappy. At this, Nehemiah recalled, "I was very much afraid." I don't think Nehemiah deliberately put on a sad face to attract the king's attention. That's the last thing he would want to do. The slightest sign of emotional stress on Nehemiah's part could make the king suspect his cupbearer's loyalty.

Nehemiah probably tried to put on a happy face around the king—but the king was such a keen judge of people that he read Nehemiah's unconscious facial cues. When the king asked Nehemiah why he was sad, Nehemiah was "very much afraid" that the king might suspect him of plotting against him. Nehemiah replied, "May the king live forever! Why should my face not look sad when the city where my ancestors are buried lies in ruins, and its gates have been destroyed by fire?"

The king asked, "What is it you want?"

At that, Nehemiah silently prayed. At critical moments, Nehemiah's first impulse was to pray. His prayer was probably a quick plea—"Lord, give me the words to say!"

Nehemiah needed heaven-sent wisdom and all the people skills he possessed if he wanted to persuade the king. "If it pleases the king," Nehemiah said, "and if your servant has found favor in his sight, let him send me to the city in Judah where my ancestors are buried so that I can rebuild it."

His choice of words is interesting—and evidence of Nehemiah's people skills. He didn't say, "Send me to Jerusalem." The city of Jerusalem had a reputation as a center of political troublemaking and revolutions. All the nations of the region had experienced conflict with Jerusalem over the centuries—the Assyrians, the Babylonians, the Egyptians, and on and on.

Nehemiah wisely avoided the word "Jerusalem" and said instead, "Send me to the city in Judah where my ancestors are buried." He appealed to the king on a personal basis rather than a political basis. Kings place a high premium on ancestry, so Nehemiah made his case in terms the king would understand—and he succeeded. As Nehemiah said in 2:6, "It pleased the king to send me; so I set a time."

Nehemiah also asked for letters of safe passage, addressed to the governors who controlled the region Nehemiah would travel through. These governors were subject to the Persian king, and these letters would guarantee that Nehemiah would be treated well along the way. The Persian king also sent officers and soldiers, representing the power and authority of the Persian Empire, to protect Nehemiah on his journey.

PEOPLE SKILLS AND THE PEOPLE OF JERUSALEM

A surgeon once said that if he had five minutes to perform a life-saving operation, he'd spend the first three minutes planning the operation. Planning is essential to success. That's why, when Nehemiah arrived in Jerusalem, his first act was to survey the situation and formulate a plan of action. Nehemiah recalled:

> I went to Jerusalem, and after staying there three days I set out during the night with a few others. I had not told anyone what my God had put in my heart to do for Jerusalem. There were no mounts with me except the one I was riding on.

> By night I went out through the Valley Gate toward the Jackal Well and the Dung Gate, examining the walls of Jerusalem, which had been broken down, and its gates, which had been destroyed by fire. Then I moved on toward the Fountain Gate and the King's Pool, but there was not enough room for my mount to get through; so I went up the valley by night, examining the wall. Finally, I turned back and reentered through the Valley Gate. The officials did not know where I had gone or what I was doing, because as yet

I had said nothing to the Jews or the priests or nobles or officials or any others who would be doing the work. (Neh. 2:11-16 NIV)

Nehemiah went out at night when the people of Jerusalem were asleep. He rode on horseback around the city and assessed the challenge of restoring the walls. Then he summoned the citizens of Jerusalem to tell them his plan. Nehemiah wrote:

Then I said to them, "You see the trouble we are in: Jerusalem lies in ruins, and its gates have been burned with fire. Come, let us rebuild the wall of Jerusalem, and we will no longer be in disgrace." I also told them about the gracious hand of my God on me and what the king had said to me.

They replied, "Let us start rebuilding." So they began this good work. (Neh. 2:17-18 NIV)

This passage, more than any other section of the Book of Nehemiah, demonstrates Nehemiah's leadership ability. He stood before all the people, laid out the problem, and called them to come together as one to solve the problem. The city lay in ruins, its gates were burned—and the people of Jerusalem were disgraced. It was time to rebuild—and God would see them through it.

I'm sure the Book of Nehemiah only gives us a brief taste of all that Nehemiah said to them that day. He undoubtedly reminded them of the glories of the past, of the golden ages of King David and King Solomon. He reminded them of the goodness and love of God. With God on their side, they could accomplish anything. Through his people skills, Nehemiah convinced the people of Jerusalem to join him in rebuilding. He got them to buy in to his vision. By the time he had finished speaking, the people shouted, without prompting from Nehemiah, "Let us start rebuilding!"

A boss might have *commanded* the people to rebuild. But Nehemiah was a leader, not a boss. He inspired and motivated and energized the people, so that *his* vision of a restored and renovated Jerusalem became *their* vision. He didn't have to order them to rebuild. They were so inspired and motivated by his message to them that he couldn't have held them back.

That is what a leader with people skills can accomplish.

Where did Nehemiah learn the art of leading through people skills? He undoubtedly honed his skills by serving as the cupbearer to the king of Persia. He had spent much of his life watching the king talking to his advisors, meeting with visiting heads of state, planning strategy, and negotiating with diplomats. Nehemiah had, in fact, been mentored by one of the most brilliant leaders in history. God had strategically placed him where he could soak up leadership wisdom from the king himself. And Nehemiah had taken all he had learned from this worldly leader, and had baptized it with the wisdom that comes only from God.

The result was that Nehemiah was a master of persuasion, negotiation, motivation, and inspiration. And he laid all these people skills before the throne of heaven and asked God to use them to accomplish His purposes. That's why the people responded with enthusiasm, "Let us start rebuilding!"

PEOPLE SKILLS FOR TIMES OF CONFLICT

Whenever leaders begin to build, there are always opponents eager to tear down. Nehemiah's opponents were named Sanballat, Tobiah, and Geshem the Arab. They had come to oppose Nehemiah and stop the rebuilding project. But Nehemiah refused to let opposition deter him from his goal. His enemies tried every trick in the book to obstruct Nehemiah, from verbal taunts to backstabbing and character assassination. Nehemiah met their obstruction head-on:

> I answered them by saying, "The God of heaven will give us success. We his servants will start rebuilding, but as for you, you have no share in Jerusalem or any claim or historic right to it." (Neh. 2:20 NIV)

If you have ever tried to achieve anything as a leader, you know people like Sanballat, Tobiah, and Geshem. You've seen their tactics and experienced their opposition. They begin with mockery and escalate from there.

One of the most important people skills a leader can possesses is the ability to let insults roll off you. The leader who must respond to every slight, every accusation, every innuendo ends up beating the air with his fists, unable to move forward. The greatest leaders in history were those who shrugged off the insults of critics, and continued moving toward their goals.

Today, we revere Abraham Lincoln for holding the Union together and ending slavery in America. But in his own time, he was viciously attacked and defamed by his enemies. Columnist Mark Bowden observed in *The Atlantic*:

> We take for granted, of course, the scornful outpouring from the Confederate states; no action Lincoln took short of capitulation would ever have quieted his southern critics. But the vituperation wasn't limited to enemies of the Union. The North was ever at his heels.... George Templeton Strong, a prominent New York lawyer and diarist, wrote that Lincoln was "a barbarian, Scythian, yahoo, or gorilla." Henry Ward

Beecher, the Connecticut-born preacher and abolitionist, often ridiculed Lincoln in his newspaper, *The Independent* (New York), rebuking him for his lack of refinement and calling him "an unshapely man." Other northern newspapers openly called for his assassination long before John Wilkes Booth pulled the trigger. He was called a coward, "an idiot," and "the original gorilla" by none other than the commanding general of his armies, George McClellan.[13]

Nehemiah didn't ignore his opponents—but he didn't obsess over them either. He answered them—once. Then he got on with the business of leading.

One of President Ronald Reagan's last acts before leaving office was to write a note to his successor, George H. W. Bush. In the note, Reagan offered a few words of encouragement and he promised to pray for Bush. The note contained only one sentence of advice: "Don't let the turkeys get you down." Mr. Reagan had lived by those words through eight years in office. He had endured enormous opposition during those years, yet he had achieved his goals of restoring the American economy and American strength around the world, and he had ended the Cold War without firing a shot.

Any leader who wants to accomplish great things must possess the people skills of knowing how to respond—or *not* respond—to opponents, critics, and complainers. There are times when you must meet opponents head on, expose falsehoods, assert your principles, and defend your record. And there are other times when you are better off pretending you didn't hear.

My good friend Chuck Daly, the late and legendary NBA coach, was famous for inventing memorable and descriptive phrases that came to be known as "Chuckisms." One of my favorite Chuckisms is the term "selective hearing." He often said, "You've gotta have selective hearing to coach in the NBA."

In the intense emotion of a game, players get fired up, and they want to stay on the floor. When Chuck was coaching the great Detroit Pistons teams of the late 1980s and early '90s, he often had to substitute players, and the player coming out of the game would often mutter, gripe, and cuss as he walked past Chuck. He learned to ignore it. He once told me, "If I react to everything I hear, I'll be in a confrontation every few minutes during the game. There are some things you just can't ignore, but I ignore most of the gripes players express in the heat of the game. My job is to help win games, not get in a showdown with my players."

The ability to respond effectively to criticism and opposition is a learned skill. You acquire it through experience, through a process of trial and error. Nehemiah handled his opponents with just the right touch—he confronted their insults, told him they had no claim or share in Jerusalem, then kept moving forward with the rebuilding project. He didn't let his opponents pull him off-course. Nehemiah set a leadership example for you and me.

MOLDING AND MOTIVATING YOUR PEOPLE

In the opening verses of Nehemiah 3, we see that everyone was motivated and involved. No one said, "I'm not getting my hands dirty! This is work that Jerusalemites won't do!" Everyone got sweaty and dirty. Everyone willingly did the grunt work and heavy lifting.

The high priest, Eliashib, and his fellow priests were the first to get dirt under their fingernails. They rebuilt the Sheep Gate and dedicated it to God. The priests of Israel were role models and spiritual leaders. They didn't hesitate to set an example for everyone else. As you read through the account, you see that everyone in Jerusalem—whether rich or poor, whether upper-class or servant class—did their part.

Women contributed to the rebuilding effort as well as men. Nehemiah 3:12 tells us, "Shallum son of Hallohesh, ruler of a half-district of Jerusalem, repaired the next section with the help of his daughters." Everyone involved in the project was a volunteer. No one was paid, and no one was drafted against their will. Everyone pitched in willingly because Nehemiah had inspired and motivated them with his people skills.

Not all the volunteers were citizens of the city. Some came from the region around Judah—cities such as Jericho, Tekoa, and Mizpah. The people of Jerusalem and the people of the villages and country-side came together and stood shoulder to shoulder. They rebuilt the walls, gates, and Temple.

Whether you lead a church, a civic organization, a corporation, a sports team, a military unit, a government agency, or the United Nations, you will find yourself leading people of different backgrounds and cultures, often with opposing political or theological views, certainly with different temperaments and emotional makeups. Somehow, you'll have to bind this wildly diverse collection of individuals into a unified and cohesive force, with everyone moving harmoniously toward a single goal.

You must become a master of such people skills as negotiation, peace-making, compromise, and conflict resolution. You must set an example of embracing and celebrating differences. You must allow each person to express his or her own individuality, while keeping the entire team focused on a common purpose. As Paul told the believers in Corinth, "The eye cannot say to the hand, 'I don't need you!' And the head cannot say to the feet, 'I don't need you!'" (1 Cor. 12:21 NIV).

Nehemiah inspired the people of Jerusalem to work together in harmony. As you read through Nehemiah 3, you see that the phrase "next to" appears more than twenty times: Zakkur was building the wall *next to* the men of Jericho, and Meshullam was making repairs *next to* Meremoth, and so on, all the way down the line. Everyone worked *next to* someone else, and as they worked, they got along with each other, they encouraged each other, they shared tools and helped each other, and in the process, they got to know and care for each other.

Working in harmony with each other, they created synergy. The result of their labor exceeded the sum of their individual efforts. Because they worked in harmony and unity, they produced an incredible amount of work in an unbelievably short period of time. Nehemiah reports that some workers vastly exceeded all expectations. For example, Hanun and the residents of Zanoah completed their assigned task, quickly repairing the Valley Gate—then they proceeded to repair an *additional* stretch of wall the length of *five football fields*. Seven times in this chapter, Nehemiah observes that this or that group repaired an additional section of the wall, over and above their assigned portion.

Because the people were motivated to work harmoniously and work extra hard, the task of repairing the city walls was completed with astonishing speed:

So the wall was completed on the twenty-fifth of Elul, in fifty-two days.

When all our enemies heard about this, all the surrounding nations were afraid and lost their self-confidence, because they realized that this work had been done with the help of our God. (Neh. 6:15-16 NIV)

Imagine—a project that should have taken months or years was completed in a mere *fifty-two days*. Through his people skills, Nehemiah inspired and motivated 99 percent of the citizens of Jerusalem to achieve the impossible.

But not 100 percent. In spite of Nehemiah's excellent people skills, there were a few people who refused to get with the program. Nehemiah called them out: "The next section was repaired by the men of Tekoa, but their nobles would not put their shoulders to the work under their supervisors" (Neh. 3:5 NIV).

There were a few so-called "nobles" who thought they were too good to do manual labor. Their names have been lost to history. Being lazy and egotistical, they missed their chance to be listed by name in God's Word for all time. Still, 99 percent participation is impressive—and a testament to Nehemiah's people skills.

PEOPLE SKILLS VS. INJUSTICE AND CORRUPTION

In Nehemiah 5, a problem arises that requires Nehemiah to bring all his people skills to bear. Strife and conflict break out within the Jerusalem community. Nehemiah investigates and finds that the cause of the conflict is greed. Nehemiah explains:

> Now the men and their wives raised a great outcry against their fellow Jews. Some were saying, "We and our sons and daughters are numerous; in order for us to eat and stay alive, we must get grain."

> Others were saying, "We are mortgaging our fields, our vineyards and our homes to get grain during the famine."

> Still others were saying, "We have had to borrow money to pay the king's tax on our fields and vineyards. Although

we are of the same flesh and blood as our fellow Jews and though our children are as good as theirs, yet we have to subject our sons and daughters to slavery. Some of our daughters have already been enslaved, but we are powerless, because our fields and our vineyards belong to others."

When I heard their outcry and these charges, I was very angry. I pondered them in my mind and then accused the nobles and officials. I told them, "You are charging your own people interest!" So I called together a large meeting to deal with them and said: "As far as possible, we have bought back our fellow Jews who were sold to the Gentiles. Now you are selling your own people, only for them to be sold back to us!" They kept quiet, because they could find nothing to say.

So I continued, "What you are doing is not right. Shouldn't you walk in the fear of our God to avoid the reproach of our Gentile enemies? I and my brothers and my men are also lending the people money and grain. But let us stop charging interest! Give back to them immediately their fields, vineyards, olive groves and houses, and also the interest you are charging them—one percent of the money, grain, new wine and olive oil."

"We will give it back," they said. "And we will not demand anything more from them. We will do as you say." (Neh. 5:1-12a NIV)

The wealthy financiers were exploiting the poor, charging such high interest rates that the poor couldn't pay their debts, and were forced to sell their children into slavery to the Gentiles. Nehemiah acted swiftly and firmly, calling a meeting of the officials and nobles, confronting them with their sin. Nehemiah also told the financiers what they had to do to make it right—and the financiers agreed to Nehemiah's terms.

Sometimes, leaders are required to deal with conflict. Sometimes, leaders must talk tough. But it takes a leader with great people skills to resolve conflict in a way that heals relationships instead of poisoning them. A leader with poor people skills might have made the problem worse, stirring up bitterness and resentment among the nobles and officials.

But Nehemiah got to the heart of the issue, which was greed and a lack of compassion for fellow Jewish citizens. He got the nobles and officials to see how wrong they had been. They sincerely repented of their mistreatment of their Jewish brothers and sisters. A boss can use threats to force people to change their behavior—but it takes a leader with people skills to persuade people to change their hearts.

Nehemiah's people skills enabled him to heal the conflict between rich and poor in Jerusalem. People skills are essential to resolving conflict and eliminating injustice within teams and organizations.

LEADERSHIP LESSONS FROM NEHEMIAH

What leadership lessons can we learn from Nehemiah, one of the great role models of people skills in the Bible?

FIRST LESSON: *Great people skills start with prayer.*

Nehemiah prayed that God would be with him, giving him wisdom, when he stood before the king of Persia to ask for an important favor. Later, Nehemiah prayed for the wisdom to lead the people in the reconstruction of Jerusalem. Again and again, throughout the Book of Nehemiah, he prays before tackling any leadership challenge—especially if there is persuasion involved.

Nehemiah may have learned people skills by watching and serving the king of Persia—but he continually prayed for God's power and wisdom in applying what he had learned. Nehemiah was persuasive and successful because he started with prayer.

SECOND LESSON: *Great leaders use people skills to inspire and motivate, so that everyone will buy into the shared vision.*
Nehemiah could not have compelled his people to achieve so much in such a short span of time through threats or intimidation. Instead, he inspired people to make *his* goal *their* goal. They worked harder than they had ever worked before because they believed in the vision of a restored, secure, and beautiful Jerusalem. He inspired and motivated the people through his people skills.

THIRD LESSON: *Great leaders don't allow opponents to sidetrack them with attacks and character assassination.*
Nehemiah was not obsessed with defending himself against his enemies. He responded to them *once*—and put them in their place. Then he ignored them and stayed focused on his goals. In the end, he didn't have to get into a shouting match with his enemies. He stayed focused on inspiring his followers, and he let the results speak for themselves. When the city wall was completed in a mere fifty-two days, his enemies had nothing more to say. The accomplishment said it all.

FOURTH LESSON: *Great leaders are visible and available.*
Nehemiah was a street-level leader—no ivory towers for him. He had calloused, dirty hands and a sweaty brow, just like the people he led. He didn't ask anyone to do anything that he wasn't willing to do himself. He was in the trenches, and people could approach him, talk to him, question him, and be inspired by him at any time during the

long workday. It was Tom Peters who urged leaders to "manage by walking around" but Nehemiah may have invented the idea.

Many of the great leaders of American history have practiced this same visible, available approach to leadership. George Washington never left his troops during the eight years of the American Revolution. And during the American Civil War, Abraham Lincoln personally visited soldiers at their camps and frontline hospitals. A tall man with an unmistakable silhouette, he made an inviting target for Confederate rifles, yet he courageously made himself visible and available.

During the early days of the War on Terror, President George W. Bush wanted to boost the morale of his soldiers in Iraq. So he decided to make a secret flight from Texas to Baghdad for Thanksgiving 2003. Only a handful of people were informed about the mission. If word got out, the flight would have to be canceled for security reasons.

President Bush left Texas aboard Air Force One, which flew under a special call sign to mask the identity of the aircraft. The distinctive blue 747 was spotted over the Atlantic by a British Airways pilot, who radioed, "Did I just see Air Force One?" The president's pilot radioed back, "Gulfstream Five." The British Airways pilot understood and kept the secret to himself.

The president's plane spiraled down to the Baghdad airport— the site of recent terror attacks. Military personnel in Baghdad were told that a USO troupe was coming aboard a C-5 cargo plane. Those who saw the president's aircraft touch down on the landing strip were amazed.

President Bush surprised hundreds of soldiers at the military mess hall at Baghdad International Airport. For two and a half hours, the President of the United States carved and served turkey, shook hands, and chatted with the soldiers. "You are defending the American people from danger," he told them, "and we are grateful."[14]

If you want to inspire and motivate your people to do their best, be visible and available to them. Share a meal with them. Talk to them. Encourage them. You'll be amazed at the influence and impact you'll have by simply spending time among your people as Nehemiah did.

FIFTH LESSON: *Great leaders are good listeners.*

We talked about the importance of listening in the chapter on communication. But good listening is also a people skill. Nehemiah listened to the problems of the poor people who were being oppressed and exploited by the financiers of Jerusalem. He listened—then he acted. He confronted those who were exploiting the poor.

Listening is a key component of problem-solving. Once, when I was a wet-behind-the-ears baseball executive in the 1960s, I became aware that a man in our farm club system was hurting our business. I went to the owner, Bob Carpenter, and told him about the problem. I didn't enjoy bringing him bad news. Telling him was one of the hardest things I ever did. But Mr. Carpenter was a good listener, and he thanked me for telling him about the problem. He added, "Why am I always the last to know?"

It's easy for leaders—even leaders with good people skills like Mr. Carpenter—to become insulated from the news they need to hear. Underlings are often reluctant to be the bearers of bad tidings. We leaders need to encourage our followers to speak up. Never make your followers afraid that you might "shoot the messenger." Keep the lines of communication open—that's a vitally important people skill.

A leader with good people skills should regularly ask, "What do you think about the situation? What would you do about it if you were in my place?" When you ask people for their opinions, they feel empowered. Their morale shoots skyward. They think, "The leader of the organization asked *my* opinion! The leader cares what *I* think! Maybe I *do* have a contribution to make."

SIXTH LESSON: *Great leaders are good delegators.*

Nehemiah divided the wall of Jerusalem into sections and assigned various groups and families to each section. He delegated authority for each section of the wall to a sub-leader for that section. The ability to delegate authority is a people skill that doesn't come naturally to everybody. Many people try to do everything themselves, either because they don't trust other people or they don't want to impose on other people.

You cannot lead if you cannot delegate. Delegating is the essence of leadership. Delegating doesn't mean handing off responsibility for a task and forgetting about it. You can delegate authority and you can delegate tasks, but you cannot delegate responsibility. You, as the leader, are still responsible for everything your people do. You must set the standards and benchmarks for their performance. You must maintain communication with your people to see that they are carrying out your overall instructions. You must accept responsibility for everything your people achieve—and accept blame when they fail.

You might say, "What if they make mistakes?" Well, I guarantee they'll make mistakes. In fact, you should *want* them to make a few mistakes, because mistakes are learning opportunities. Don't punish honest mistakes. If you make people afraid to make mistakes, they will learn to play it safe, cover up errors, and shift the blame. Instead, encourage your followers to learn the lessons of their mistakes—and consider it an investment in their growth and training.

SEVENTH LESSON: *Great leaders level with their followers.*

Nehemiah always spoke to the people candidly, honestly, and straight from the shoulder. He leveled with them about the enormity of the challenges they faced, about the threats arrayed against them, about the insults hurled at them by their enemies. By leveling with the people, by telling them the unvarnished truth, he made them understand their desperate situation. They responded to Nehemiah's straight talk by expending an unbelievable effort—and completing the project in fifty-two days.

All too often, leaders are tempted to sugarcoat the truth, to hide the bad news, to give their followers happy talk instead of honest information. Just as Churchill told the people of Great Britain in World War II, "I have nothing to offer you but blood, toil, tears, and sweat," Nehemiah leveled with the people of Jerusalem about the blood, toil, tears, and sweat needed to restore the walls and gates of the city. Were the people of Jerusalem discouraged by Nehemiah's message? No, they were energized and empowered to work harder than they had ever worked in their lives.

Sam Walton, the founder of Walmart, once said, "Communicate everything you possibly can to your partners [Sam's word for employees]. The more they know, the more they'll understand. The more they understand, the more they'll care. Once they care, there's no stopping them."[15]

To lead like to Nehemiah, build the Third Side of Leadership into your leadership life. Practice and improve your people skills. What are the walls you want to build? What are the obstacles you want to overcome? Begin with prayer—then inspire and motivate your people to believe in themselves and reach for your vision.

Then turn them loose and watch them achieve miracles.

CHAPTER 4: QUESTIONS FOR REFLECTION AND DISCUSSION

1. Nehemiah needed excellent people skills to make a request of the King of Persia, to organize and lead the rebuilding effort in Jerusalem, to keep his people motivated, and to deal with conflict and persecution from his enemies. How did Nehemiah learn or acquire his people skills?

   What are your strongest people skills? What are your weak areas? What lessons do you learn from Nehemiah and how can you apply those insights to strengthen yourself in those weak areas?

2. Nehemiah had to bring together people from different social and economic classes, different cultural backgrounds, different personality types, and different generations; then he had to form them into a cohesive, unified force for rebuilding the city. Why are people skills important for bringing unity out of diversity?

   Have you ever had to bring diverse types of people together to form a unified team or organization? Were you successful? Why or why not? What insights do you draw from Nehemiah to help you bridge the differences between people on your team?

3. In Nehemiah 5, conflict and strife arise. Nehemiah must summon his people skills to heal a widening division between groups within his community. What people skills do you see Nehemiah bringing to bear in this situation?

   Think of a time when you had to deal with conflict in your organization or on your team. Were you successful in healing that division? What people skills did you use to help solve that conflict? What leadership insights do you learn from the example of Nehemiah?

4. Nehemiah was a visible, available leader. He led by walking around. He also led by example, getting down in the trenches with his people and getting his hands dirty. What would happen if you spent more time with your troops, doing some of the grunt work right alongside them? What are some specific ways you could become more visible and available to the people you lead?

5. Nehemiah shows us that listening skills are not only good communication skills but also good people skills. How might you and your people benefit if you improved your listening skills? What actions can you take to become a more effective listener?

6. Great leaders are great delegators. If you can't delegate, you can't lead. On a scale of 1 to 10, how good a delegator are you?

What are the issues and attitudes that prevent you from being a more effective delegator? What lessons can you learn from Nehemiah that would help you to become the kind of delegator and leader you ought to be?

Do you find it hard to "let go" and allow people the freedom to make their own decisions, including their own mistakes? If yes, what steps do you need to take to better empower the people you lead, and give them the freedom to exercise their own initiative and creativity?

JOSEPH: A LEADER OF FLAWLESS CHARACTER

I've written four books on the character traits and leadership principles of the late UCLA basketball coach John Wooden. In the process, I interviewed literally hundreds of people who knew Coach Wooden. During those interviews, I noticed a consistent pattern: almost every person I talked to remarked about the flawless character of Coach Wooden.

Here was a coach who achieved ten NCAA national championships, including seven in a row plus an 88-game winning streak. Six times he was named National Coach of the Year. But his achievements were of secondary importance to those who knew him. What really impressed people about Coach Wooden was his sterling character.

I got to know Coach Wooden during the last ten years of his life, and I can tell you that I've never met anyone like him. He was unique.

One of Coach Wooden's former student managers explained his character to me in these words: "The John Wooden on the practice floor was the same John Wooden in the locker room, and the John Wooden in the locker room was the same John Wooden on the campus at UCLA, and the John Wooden on the campus was the same John Wooden at home. He didn't change from place to place and situation to situation. There was an absolute consistency and integrity to his life."

A leader of flawless character is someone whose walk and talk are in complete alignment. Such leaders demand absolute integrity of themselves and their followers. Leaders of flawless character don't merely resist temptation when it comes—they build firewalls in their lives to keep temptation far away.

Dr. Billy Graham, in his autobiography, told the story of how he and other leaders in his organization took proactive steps to make sure they would never bring shame upon themselves, their families, or the gospel. In 1948, Dr. Graham and his leadership team—Cliff Barrows, Grady Wilson, and George Beverly Shea—drove to Modesto, California, for a series of evangelistic meetings. Dr. Graham wrote:

> From time to time Cliff, Bev, Grady, and I talked among ourselves about the recurring problems many evangelists seemed to have, and about the poor image so-called mass evangelism had in the eyes of many people....
>
> One afternoon during the Modesto meetings, I called the Team together to discuss the problem. Then I asked them to go to their rooms for an hour and list all the problems they could think of that evangelists and evangelism encountered.
>
> When they returned, the lists were remarkably similar, and in a short amount of time, we made a series of resolutions or commitments among ourselves that would guide us in our future evangelistic work.[16]

Dr. Graham and his team resolved that they would never manipulate audiences through emotional appeals, never exaggerate successes, and never misuse the funds that had been entrusted to them. The most important commitment of all may have been their resolution regarding their moral integrity. "We pledged among ourselves," Dr.

Graham wrote, "to avoid any situation that would have even the appearance of compromise or suspicion. From that day on, I did not travel, meet, or eat alone with a woman other than my wife."

That pledge became known as The Modesto Manifesto, and it enabled these Christian leaders to ensure, once and for all, that "integrity would be the hallmark of both our lives and our ministry."[17] Over the seven-decade history of the Billy Graham Evangelistic Association, there has never been a hint of scandal surrounding the leadership of that organization. Other religious leaders and organizations have fallen into disgrace during that time, but the Graham organization has maintained a reputation for flawless integrity. Why? Because the leadership circle of the organization made a commitment to build moral firewalls between themselves and temptation.

This kind of integrity used to be applauded in our society. Lately, some pundits have tried to turn integrity into a crime. For example, a March 2017 *Washington Post* story mentioned that Vice President Mike Pence has followed the "Billy Graham rule" throughout his marriage. He has vowed never to be alone or dine alone with a woman who is not his wife. After the report in the *Washington Post* appeared, Pence—who is an outspoken Christian—was widely condemned and ridiculed in the media.

A writer in *The New Yorker* claimed that Pence's moral policy was an attack on equality for women. A man could have a private business lunch with Pence, but a woman was denied the same advantage. According to the writer, the vice president's moral principles made it "well-nigh impossible [for him] to view a group of people [women] as fully human."[18]

Another writer, Glennon Doyle Melton, wrote in *Time*, "Pence's rule for his marriage perpetuates religious and political ideologies based on false, dehumanizing ideologies about women that, when espoused by those in power, have manifested disastrous outcomes for all of us. If Pence cannot eat alone with a woman, it must be because when he sees a woman across a table, she's not an adviser, she's not a teacher, she's not a leader, she's not a constituent—she is only a sexual entity."[19]

These are ridiculous arguments. How difficult is it to simply have a third person present at a business lunch? I can't believe Pence's moral principles have prevented anyone from advancing in their career, nor caused anyone to feel not "fully human." Pence's moral stance is not an attack on women. On the contrary, it's his way of *respecting* all women, especially his wife Karen.

Pence is eliminating not only temptation, but even the *appearance* of impropriety. He is also obeying God's Word, which says, "Abstain from all appearance of evil" (1 Thess. 5:22 KJV). He is protecting his own reputation and the reputation of any women he might have conversations with by maintaining this moral firewall. I consider these firewalls essential for people in leadership, especially Christian leaders, because there are always people trying to take us down and destroy our influence. This doesn't mean our opponents won't lie about us, but why make their job easier by creating the appearance of impropriety?

If our opponents can't find a flaw in our character, they'll try to use our own moral integrity against us, as they have with Pence. But God will vindicate us if we maintain our good character. That's the lesson we learn from the life of an Old Testament leader named Joseph.

A YOUNG MAN OF GODLY CHARACTER

More space is devoted to the story of Joseph than to any other character in the Book of Genesis. It's the story of a young man whose flawless character elevates him to a leadership role on the world stage. The story begins in Genesis 37.

Joseph was the eleventh of Jacob's twelve sons. There was constant sibling rivalry among the sons of Jacob. Jacob unwisely fueled the dissension in his family by showing favoritism toward Joseph, symbolized by a gift of a beautiful robe, embroidered in many colors.

When Joseph was seventeen, he had two dreams, and he told these dreams to his father and brothers. In the first dream, which took place during the grain harvest, Joseph's brothers' sheaves of grain bowed down to Joseph's sheaf of grain. In the second dream, the sun, moon, and eleven stars bowed down to Joseph. These dreams were not hard for the brothers to interpret. His dreams suggested that Joseph would one day rule over his brothers, and they would be subject to his authority. These dreams gave the brothers even more reason to hate Joseph—and they began to plot his murder.

One day, the brothers were in the fields with their flocks when they saw Joseph approaching. "Here comes that dreamer!" they said. "Come now, let's kill him and throw him into one of these cisterns and say that a ferocious animal devoured him. Then we'll see what comes of his dreams."

As Joseph approached, the brothers seized him, took his robe, and tossed him into a cistern. Then they sat down and ate their meal. Soon they saw a trading caravan on its way to Egypt. One of Joseph's brothers suggested selling him into slavery. The brothers pulled Joseph out of the cistern and sold him to the slave-traders for twenty pieces of silver, and Joseph was led away, a captive and a slave.

The slave-traders sold Joseph to an Egyptian official named Potiphar. Because of Joseph's flawless character, Potiphar soon elevated Joseph, making him chief of his staff of servants. Unfortunately, Potiphar had a wife who couldn't be trusted. She continually tried to seduce Joseph—but Joseph had wisely set up moral firewalls in his life. He refused to betray his employer's trust.

Joseph's answer to Potiphar's wife was, "No one is greater in this house than I am. My master has withheld nothing from me except you, because you are his wife. How then could I do such a wicked thing and sin against God?" (Gen. 39:9 NIV). This statement packs a lot of information. It tells us that Joseph's flawless character enabled him to rise to the top position in Potiphar's household—none of Potiphar's servants had more authority than him. As a result, Joseph enjoyed many privileges—every privilege, in fact, except Potiphar's wife.

Genesis goes on to tell us, "And though she spoke to Joseph day after day, he refused to go to bed with her or even be with her" (Gen. 39:10 NIV). This woman was persistent! She tried to seduce Joseph *every day*. And Joseph followed the Billy Graham and Mike Pence rule—he refused to even be in the same room with her.

Joseph's rejection of her advances filled her with rage. Finally, she decided that if she couldn't seduce him, she would destroy him. She accused Joseph of raping her—and though Potiphar probably knew she was lying, he couldn't take Joseph's word over his wife's. So Potiphar threw Joseph into prison.

Now, it might seem that Joseph was being punished for his good character—and, in a way, he was. We often pay a price in the short run to maintain our integrity, though integrity always pays off in the long run. Would Joseph have gone to prison if he had yielded to this woman's temptation? We don't know. Perhaps Potiphar's wife would have had her fun with Joseph, then accused him anyway—just to be rid of him. In that case, Joseph would have still gone to prison—and he would have deserved it. Though Joseph paid a price for his integrity, his integrity was worth the price.

Even in prison, God was with Joseph. God gave him an opportunity to do a favor for one of his fellow prisoners. The prisoner had a dream, and Joseph interpreted it. This man had been the cupbearer of Pharaoh. After Joseph interpreted the dream, the cupbearer promised to help Joseph if he got out of prison. A few days later, the man was released from prison—but instead of keeping his promise, he forgot Joseph and got on with his life.

Two years passed. God caused Pharaoh to experience two disturbing dreams. When Pharaoh awoke from the dreams, he was terrified. He summoned his wise men and demanded that they tell him the meaning of the dreams—but no one could interpret them. Finally, Joseph's prison friend, the cupbearer, remembered how Joseph had interpreted his dream. The cupbearer told Pharaoh about Joseph.

Pharaoh's guards took Joseph out of prison, and brought him before Pharaoh. After hearing the dream, Joseph told Pharaoh that Egypt would experience seven prosperous years followed by seven years of famine. Joseph offered a solution to the coming famine: Egypt must store up some of its grain harvest during the seven years of abundance so that the people would have food to eat during the coming famine.

Pharaoh was amazed at Joseph's wisdom. Though Joseph was only thirty years old, a Hebrew fresh from prison, Pharaoh made him the second most powerful official in the Egyptian government. Joseph answered only to Pharaoh himself. The ruler of Egypt put a signet ring on Joseph's finger, placed a gold chain around his neck, and dressed him in royal robes.

The prophetic dreams Joseph told his brothers in Canaan were fulfilled in the land of Egypt. Joseph became a powerful leader in Egypt, and he wielded authority over the brothers who had sold him into slavery. Joseph's character was tested by sexual temptation, lying accusations, false imprisonment, and a prison "friend" who forgot him and neglected him for years. Throughout his trials and tribulations, Joseph maintained his flawless character. Many people would have been embittered by his experiences, but Joseph never stopped trusting God. It takes enormous character strength to endure injustice without complaining. Joseph's character was the key to his future as a leader.

A BRIEF LIST OF ESSENTIAL CHARACTER QUALITIES

Here are just a few of the character qualities we see in the life of Joseph—character qualities that are essential for our lives if we want to be complete as leaders in any arena of life:

Integrity: This comes first on any list of character qualities. Integrity means being morally whole and uncompartmentalized. A leader of integrity is the same person, behaving the same way, whether at home or work or church, whether in front of a crowd or in absolute privacy. The opposite of integrity is hypocrisy. If your followers believe you have integrity, they will trust you and follow you anywhere. The moment your integrity is compromised, their trust in you will evaporate. As General Richard B. Myers once told me, "Credibility comes from character—and especially from the character trait called *integrity.*" Joseph distinguished himself as a leader of integrity.

Diligence: Also called a "work ethic," diligences and eagerness to work hard and achieve excellence. A diligent leader is a self-starter, a hard worker, and a fanatic about quality. "Good enough" is never good enough for a diligent leader. Diligent people don't work hard merely as a means to success. They believe that a strong work ethic is morally good, and that laziness is a sin. Great leaders don't *demand* diligence of their followers as much as they *inspire* diligence in their followers by the example they set. Joseph's diligent leadership led Potiphar to place him in authority over his entire household.

Honesty: This character quality may be defined as an uncompromising commitment to the truth. An honest person is willing to pay the price of telling the truth. Honest leaders admit their own mistakes. They tell the truth on their tax returns. They never lie in their advertising claims or product labeling. Honesty builds trust, because trust is based on truth. Joseph's impeccable honesty won the trust of the Egyptian Pharaoh.

Patience: Leaders tend to be impatient by nature, so a patient leader will stand out from the crowd. Patience is the willingness to trust God's timing and be at peace while waiting. Joseph demonstrated patience as a slave in Potiphar's household, and as a prisoner, forgotten by his friend, the cupbearer. God rewarded Joseph's patience by elevating him to a place of leadership and influence in the Egyptian government.

Humility: The character quality of humility does not mean self-abasement or self-contempt. It is simply having a realistic view of oneself and others. A humble leader can be confident without being arrogant. A humble leader can balance self-respect with a respect for others. A humble leader is immune to both flattery and insult. As Mother Teresa once said, "If you are humble, nothing can touch you, neither praise nor disgrace, because you know who you are." Joseph never allowed circumstances or other people to determine his sense of self-worth. In every circumstance, he maintained his humility.

Self-discipline: A self-disciplined leader masters his or her behavior and impulses, and is not a slave to bad habits. Self-disciplined leaders demonstrate good time-management habits, and maintain a healthy and balanced lifestyle. It was Joseph's self-discipline that enabled him to withstand a daily barrage of sexual temptation from Potiphar's wife. Leaders who lack self-discipline may get away with sins and bad habits for a while—but they tend to destroy themselves over time.

Perseverance: Nothing of lasting importance is ever achieved without perseverance. The path of leadership is strewn with obstacles and opposition. Leaders who achieve greatness are those who simply won't quit, who cannot be stopped. Again and again in his life, Joseph faced obstacles and opposition—and he persevered through it all until he achieved his goals.

Faith: Leaders of faith are willing to live and act in accordance with the commandments and promises of God. Faith is trusting in God. Joseph endured betrayal, enslavement, injustice, false accusation, false imprisonment, and more—yet he never let go of his trust in God. Joseph was a leader of faith. He is a role model of faith for you and me.

There are many other character traits we could discuss—fairness, tolerance, compassion, unselfishness, rationality, dignity, loyalty, responsibility, and more. Joseph possessed all of these character qualities in abundance. He was a leader of flawless character—and an example of character-based leadership for you and me.

THE SUFFERINGS OF JOSEPH

Joseph suffered greatly—not as a punishment for sin, but for living a godly life. Joseph endured injustice—and as the apostle Paul told his spiritual protégé Timothy, "Everyone who wants to live a godly life in Christ Jesus will be persecuted" (2 Tim. 3:12 NIV). Godliness is no guarantee of a life of ease. In fact, the godliest people in the world are often in all kinds of trouble. Yet God is always with us when we endure persecution for His sake. He will comfort us, defend us, and deliver us if we place our trust in Him.

Genesis closes with the conclusion of the story of Joseph: "So Joseph died at the age of a hundred and ten. And after they embalmed him, he was placed in a coffin in Egypt" (Gen. 50:26 NIV).

That's the end of the life of Joseph—but it's not the end of the story of Joseph. He dies, he is embalmed, he is placed in a coffin in Egypt—but the story continues in the Book of Exodus. There, after the slow passage of four centuries, God uses a man named Moses to deliver the people of Israel from the land of Egypt. They will take the coffin with the bones of Joseph, and by the supernatural power of God they will carry Joseph's remains out of Egypt and into the promised land. He will return to the land of Canaan, where he first dreamed his big dreams.

Everybody dies. Everyone must pass through the doorway of death to reach eternity. Everyone must be delivered from this valley of the shadow of death, just as the remains of Joseph were delivered out of Egypt and carried into Canaan. God has given us this great hope, that after we have served him and loved him and committed our lives to him, he will rescue us from our mortal corruption and take us into the eternal land he has promised to us.

Joseph is our role model. He is an example of what it means to trust God, what it means to live a life of flawless character, and what it means to achieve the leadership vision God has given us. Joseph suffered mistreatment, testing, temptation, and injustice. He knew what it meant to be enslaved. He knew what it meant to be exalted.

Through it all, his faith never wavered, his character never crumbled. He was consistent in good times and bad, in the prison and in the palace, in the sunshine and in the darkness.

Joseph is the greatest example in the Old Testament of character that does not break under pressure, character without flaw, character that endures. Joseph is one of the best examples I know of a leader who exemplifies the Fourth Side of Leadership: Character. There is no other hero of the Bible, other than Jesus Himself, who better exemplifies consistent, flawless character.

Most evangelical Bible scholars consider Joseph a symbolic Old Testament type of Jesus Christ. There are many points of similarity. Joseph was loved by his father Jacob, just as Jesus was loved by God the father. Joseph was rejected by his brothers and sold into slavery for twenty pieces of silver, much as Jesus was rejected by his brothers and sold for thirty pieces of silver. Joseph, like Jesus, was a "suffering servant." He was tempted, yet without sin. He descended into the pit and the prison cell, and was raised triumphant. Like Jesus, Joseph forgave his brothers for their mistreatment of him, and God used Joseph to save his brothers from death.

Joseph is also a symbolic embodiment of godly leadership. His flawless character earned him the trust and approval of his master, Potiphar. His flawless character earned him the friendship of the cupbearer in prison, so that Joseph had a friend in high places when Pharaoh needed an interpreter of dreams. His flawless character earned him the trust of the ruler of all Egypt, and positioned him to wield power and authority in Egypt—the land he had first entered as a chattel slave.

Joseph was seventeen years old when he was sold into slavery. He was thirty years old when he was elevated to the position of leadership by Pharaoh. How long did Joseph spend in obscurity, in slavery, suffering injustice because of what his brothers had done to him? Answer: thirteen years. As you read these words, you may have been enduring a long period of insecurity, injustice, and suffering. You may have experienced setbacks through no fault of your own. You may have even been persecuted for your godly witness and righteous behavior.

If you have suffered unfairly, if you have endured years of obscurity, then take comfort in this: You are in good company. You are in the company of Joseph, the leader of flawless character. It may well be that God is taking you through a valley of obscurity, a trial of injustice—not because God wants to hurt you, but because He wants to teach you, grow you, increase your faith, and deepen your character.

As the apostle Paul once wrote, "Not only so, but we also glory in our sufferings, because we know that suffering produces perseverance; perseverance, character; and character, hope. And hope does not put us to shame, because God's love has been poured out into our hearts through the Holy Spirit, who has been given to us" (Rom. 5:3-5 NIV).

If you find yourself in a pit because you have disobeyed God and received the consequences of your disobedience, then learn the lesson of the pit. Confess your sins, turn to God, and seek forgiveness. But if you find yourself in a pit through no fault of your own, or because you are being persecuted for following God, then allow God to deepen your Christian character, increase your faith, and make you more like Christ.

We tend to think that a life of ease and comfort should be our reward for obeying God and doing his will. But that's not true. The Bible teaches that believers frequently suffer persecution as a result of living godly lives. The apostles suffered persecution. The early church suffered persecution. Christians around the world are suffering persecution all the time. Why should you and I be exempt?

Joseph was not focused on having an easy, comfortable life. Joseph was not focused on accumulating wealth and building a secure retirement fund. Joseph was not focused on worldly success and fame. He was focused on obeying God and maintaining the purity of his character. And sometimes, he paid a price for his integrity. The lesson of Joseph's life is that integrity is worth the price.

Do you want to be a complete leader, a leader of flawless character? If so, then Joseph is the template for your leadership life. What are some of the leadership lessons we can learn from Joseph, this hero of flawless character?

FIRST LESSON: *A great leadership vision cannot be achieved without excellent character.*

God gave Joseph two dreams, two visions of the future. Joseph couldn't understand all that those two visions meant. He didn't know, before those visions could be fulfilled, he'd undergo several acid tests of character.

You may have a leadership vision that God has given to you. There will probably be obstacles, opposition, and suffering in your path before you achieve that vision. You may suffer betrayal and injustice on your way to fulfilling that vision. Don't worry about the future. If Joseph had known all that lay ahead of him, he might have given up while he was still in the cistern. As someone once said, God made the world round so that we could not see over the horizon.

All you need to know is this: If God has given you a leadership vision, you'll need excellent character to achieve it. You'll need moral firewalls to protect you from temptation. You'll need an intense and unwavering faith, seamless integrity, total honesty, great patience and much more. The Fourth Side of Leadership is essential to achieving your grand leadership vision.

SECOND LESSON: *Leaders should expect to be misunderstood, betrayed, and treated unfairly.*

Your leadership vision will inspire and attract some people to follow you—but it will rub other people the wrong way. Some, like Joseph's brothers, may be jealous of you and may attack you. But if you are convinced God has given you this vision, then summon the character strength to see it through to completion. Don't give up on the vision God has given you.

Joseph's brothers thought his dreams were self-aggrandizing predictions that he would exalt himself—and they would be humiliated. They didn't understand that these dreams came directly from God, and represented a brighter future for all of them. They didn't know that Joseph would one day save their lives in a time of famine. Similarly, the people who oppose you may misinterpret your vision as a threat to their future.

If people oppose you, don't give in to anger or resentment. Continue to love them and forgive them. Reach out—and you may win them over. Whether they come around or not, keep moving forward, keep trusting in God, keep pursuing your vision.

THIRD LESSON: *Great leaders maintain strong firewalls against temptation.*

Don't flirt with temptation. Don't compromise. Don't yield. Keep temptation as far away as possible. Make a decision ahead of time, then stick to it—just like Billy Graham, just like Mike Pence, just like Joseph. If you leave the slightest gap in your moral armor, temptation will find a way to your heart. Your character must be unbreakable. Your firewall must be impenetrable.

FOURTH LESSON: *Leaders of flawless character are patient with God's timetable.*

Some godly leaders seem to find their vision and mission in life at an early age. Other godly leaders seem to spend years in obscurity, undergoing adversity, enduring times of frustration and immobility. They ask, "God, why am I in this desert, this prison? Why is my leadership vision locked away? Why am I sidelined?" These are questions Joseph surely asked himself during his time of enslavement and imprisonment. He must've wondered, "God, what were those visions about? Why did you show me dreams of sheaves of wheat and the moon and the stars bowing to me? What did that mean? How long are you going to leave me in this prison for a crime I never committed?"

God's timetable is not a one-size-fits-all proposition. Your journey will not be the same as mine, and mine will not be the same as the next person's journey. When you start to grow impatient with your time of testing and learning and growing, remember Joseph. Remember his thirteen years of unjust adversity. And remember that God, in his wisdom and good time, elevated Joseph and used him in a mighty way.

Your time is coming. Trust God. Be patient with His timetable.

FIFTH LESSON: *Leaders of excellent character are people who forgive.*

Joseph suffered incredible mistreatment because of the jealousy of his brothers. Yet Joseph forgave them, loved them, and cared for them. Joseph saved their lives.

Great leaders know the value of forgiveness. Joseph was a forerunner of the One who said, "Father, forgive them, for they don't know what they are doing." Joseph teaches us what character looks like, what leadership looks like, and what forgiveness looks like. Emulate the character of Joseph and practice the forgiveness of Joseph. Guard your character with a firewall of wisdom and integrity.

BE A LEADER WHO FORGIVES

In the early morning hours of April 18, 1942, Army Corporal Jacob DeShazer took off aboard a B-25 bomber from the aircraft carrier *Hornet*. He was the bombardier, part of a five-man flight crew. There were sixteen bombers in the flight group for this one-way mission—and the planes couldn't carry enough fuel to return to the *Hornet*. DeShazer's plane would drop its bombs on Tokyo, then fly on to China where the crew would bail out.

After hours of tense flying toward the Japanese mainland, Jake DeShazer's plane approached the target. He released the bombs. Below and behind him, factories exploded. Anti-aircraft fire perforated the skin of the plane. Somehow, they made it to China, and the crew bailed out—but they were over Japanese-held territory.

DeShazer broke several ribs when he landed. He was quickly captured and taken to a prison camp, where he spent many months in a concrete cell that baked like an oven in the summer, and chilled like a deep freeze in winter. He was sick with dysentery much of the time, and was cruelly mistreated by the guards. After two years, his captors allowed the prisoners to share a single Bible. Each man would have the Bible for three weeks, then pass it to the next man. He read straight through the Old and New Testaments, and concentrated on memorizing the words of Jesus.

One day, the guard viciously slammed the door on DeShazer's foot. As DeShazer grasped his throbbing foot, he felt hatred for the guard. Then the words of Jesus came to him: "Love your enemies and ask God to bless those who persecute you."

The next day, the guard bought Jake DeShazer his meager ration of food. DeShazer greeted the guard with a blessing in Japanese, then asked the man about his family. The guard was astonished at Jake's kindness. Later, the guard brought Jake an extra ration of food and a piece of candy. The random acts of cruelty stopped.

In August 1945, the war ended, and Jake DeShazer was released. By learning to forgive his prison guard, Jake developed a love for the Japanese people. After the war, he returned to Japan with his wife, Florence, and they served in Japan as missionaries.

DeShazer shared Christ with a man named Mitsuo Fuchida, and this man accepted Christ as his Lord and Savior. Jake later discovered that Fuchida was the flight commander who led the Japanese attack on Pearl Harbor. Because of Jake's witness, Fuchida became an Evangelist, and became known as "the Billy Graham of Japan."

One of the most important character qualities a leader must have is the trait of forgiveness. Forgiveness characterized the leadership life of both Joseph and Jesus. Forgiveness changed the life of Jacob DeShazer and Mitsuo Fuchida. Countless people found eternal life through Jesus Christ because Jacob DeShazer made a decision to follow Christ and forgive his prison guard.

To be a leader of excellent character, be a leader who forgives.

CHAPTER 5: QUESTIONS FOR REFLECTION AND DISCUSSION

1. Joseph was a young man of sterling character. When his employer's wife tried to seduce him, he steadfastly maintained his integrity. The woman falsely accused him of rape and had him thrown into prison. If that is what happens when a young leader maintains his integrity, how can we be sure that good character is a leadership asset? Wasn't Joseph's good character actually a liability in that situation? Explain.

2. Joseph's character qualities included: integrity, diligence, honesty, patience, humility, self-discipline, perseverance, and faith. Which of these traits was most important to his leadership success?

   Which of the traits listed above are you strongest in? Weakest in? What steps can you take to grow and improve in the weaker areas of your character?

3. Think of a time when your character as a leader was tested. Did you pass the test as Joseph did? Or did you fall short?

   What lessons in leadership character can you learn from the example of Joseph? What steps can you take to become a leader of impeccable character like Joseph?

4. Joseph spent thirteen years as either a slave or a prisoner, then God elevated him to a position of leadership under Pharaoh. Do you identify with Joseph? Are you enduring a long period of obscurity, suffering, or injustice? Have you experienced setbacks in your profession through no fault of your own?

Do you find it hard to be patient with God's timetable? How does the story of Joseph encourage or motivate you to keep persevering through tough times?

5. The Bible teaches that believers often suffer persecution as a direct result of their godly way of life. How do you feel about that? Does it seem unfair? Does it trouble you? Or does it encourage you to know that other believers are suffering the same opposition and trials you are enduring?

6. Great leaders maintain firewalls against temptation. Have you put moral and spiritual firewalls in place to protect you from temptation? Describe them. Are you sure they're adequate?

   What additional steps should you take to guard your character and reputation against a scandal or moral breakdown?

7. Great leaders understand the importance of forgiveness. Is there anyone in your life who needs your forgiveness? Is there anyone in your life who has a grievance against you? What steps will you take this week to forgive or be forgiven?

CHAPTER 6

KING DAVID: COMPETENT TO LEAD

When Hurricane Katrina howled ashore late Sunday night on August 29, 2005, it cut a trail of devastation along the Gulf Coast from Texas to the Florida Panhandle. The fury of the hurricane tested the competency of leaders at every level of government. Again and again throughout the crisis, leadership failed the test.

An estimated 1,800 people died, many of them needlessly. The National Weather Service, the Coast Guard, and the National Hurricane Center provided excellent tracking of the hurricane, and government officials had plenty of time to prepare. But leadership seemed either paralyzed or unaware of the peril—and the response of government was late and inadequate.

The mayor's office did not issue an order to evacuate until it was too late—until Amtrak had already moved its passenger trains out of the city and the airlines had evacuated their airplanes. The city could have evacuated thousands aboard school buses, but chose not to because of insurance concerns and a shortage of drivers. When the levees broke, five hundred school buses were flooded and destroyed.

The federal response was frequently inadequate and often completely wrongheaded. For example, medical supplies donated to hurricane-damaged Methodist Hospital in New Orleans were confiscated by FEMA bureaucrats. Hundreds of patients were stranded at the hospital without food, medicine, or power—and a dozen patients died in the 110-degree heat.[20] When TV news cameras showed President Bush commending FEMA director Michael Brown ("Brownie, you're doing a heck of a job"), the president appeared to be out of touch with the realities on the ground. A CNN report blamed the bungled response on "a leadership vacuum" and "bureaucratic red tape."[21]

A major natural disaster has a way of exposing incompetent leadership at every level. The rollout of a massive new federal program can also expose incompetent leadership.

In October 2013, the federal government unveiled its new website, HealthCare.gov, to provide insurance to previously uninsured Americans under the Affordable Care Act (a.k.a. Obamacare). By the time the website was launched, the price tag for the website had reached more than $500 million (after one year of operation, the Office of the Inspector General reported that those costs had topped $1.7 billion). Major American corporations such as Apple, Amazon, and eBay maintain websites that are far more complicated, serve hundreds of millions of users, and were created at a tiny fraction of the cost of HealthCare.gov.

What's more, the Apple, Amazon, and eBay websites work. In fact, they work brilliantly. When HealthCare.gov was launched, it crashed—repeatedly. It didn't work at all.

People found it impossible to navigate the HealthCare.gov website. Insurance companies reported that the HealthCare.gov servers sent them incomplete or duplicate applications, making it impossible to sign people up for coverage. Private patient information, including Social Security numbers, were not secured by the website and could easily be hacked. Health and Human Services

Secretary Kathleen Sebelius, who was in charge of administering the website, admitted that convicted felons might have been hired to assist patients—and could have access to sensitive patient information.[22]

Daniel Levinson, the Health and Human Services Inspector General, concluded that a lack of competent leadership "caused delays in decision-making, lack of clarity in project tasks, and the inability of [government agencies] to recognize the magnitude of problems as the project deteriorated.... Leadership and staff took little action to respond to warnings."[23]

When government agencies and programs fail, incompetent leadership is usually to blame. Julius Caesar once said, "Every soldier has a right to competent command." I would add that every taxpayer has a right to competent government leadership. Every stockholder, stakeholder, and customer has a right to competent corporate leadership. Every church member has a right to competent church leadership. Every player on every team has a right to competent coaching leadership.

An incompetent leader cannot earn trust. An incompetent leader cannot move an organization toward its vision. An incompetent leader is not truly a leader at all. That's why the Fifth Side of Leadership Is *Competence*. Where do we find authentic competent leadership? We find it in the Bible, in the person of Israel's most famous ruler, King David.

COMPETENT TO UNITE A NATION

The book of 2 Samuel describes the government of King David, and shows how he divided his administration into departments with executives in charge of various functions of government: "David reigned over all Israel, doing what was just and right for all his people.

Joab son of Zeruiah was over the army; Jehoshaphat son of Ahilud was recorder; Zadok son of Ahitub and Ahimelek son of Abiathar were priests; Seraiah was secretary; Benaiah son of Jehoiada was over the Kerethites and Pelethites; and David's sons were priests" (2 Sam. 8:15-18 NIV).

Here we see a picture of competent administration that has been carefully structured, so that the needs of the people can be effectively met. The most important needs of the people involved protection from Israel's enemies and maintaining the spiritual health of the nation.

Theologian W. M. Taylor made this observation on the leadership competence of King David: "In the minds of most readers of the Bible, the name of David, king of Israel, is associated mainly with military prowess, poetic genius, and personal piety; and only on the rarest occasions do we hear any reference made to his administrative ability. Yet in this last quality he was at least as remarkable as in any one of the others; and great injustice is done to him if we leave out of view the eminent services which he rendered to his country by the exercise of his governmental and organizing faculties.... More than Charlemagne did for Europe, or Alfred for England, David accomplished for the tribes of Israel."[24]

David was the second king over the kingdom of Israel and Judah. Israel's first king, Saul, repeatedly disobeyed God's instructions, offering an unlawful sacrifice (1 Sam. 13:8-14 NIV), and confiscating the property of the Amalekites after God ordered him to destroy their property (1 Sam. 15 NIV). Because of his disobedience, the prophet Samuel told Saul, "You have done a foolish thing. You have not kept the command the Lord your God gave you; if you had, he would have established your kingdom over Israel for all time. But now your kingdom will not endure; the Lord has sought out a man after his own heart and appointed him ruler of his people, because you have not kept the Lord's command."

That phrase, "the Lord has sought out a man after his own heart," is significant because it refers to David—even though Samuel didn't know it when he spoke those words. As the apostle Paul affirmed in Acts 13:22, "After removing Saul, he made David their king. God testified concerning him: 'I have found David son of Jesse, a man after my own heart; he will do everything I want him to do.'"

In 1 Samuel 16, after God rejected Saul as king, God sent Samuel to anoint David, the youngest son of Jesse of Bethlehem, as Israel's future king. From that day on, God's Spirit was with David in a powerful way. King Saul, meanwhile, was tormented, because God's Spirit had departed from him. Saul sent his servants to find a musician whose music could soothe his soul—and the musician they found was David. So David entered the service of King Saul, and he became best friends with Saul's son Jonathan.

In 1 Samuel 17, the Philistines gathered to make war against Israel, and selected a champion named Goliath. When no one else in Israel dared to stand against Goliath, David stepped forward. Saul wanted to put his own armor on David, but David rejected the armor, choosing to face Goliath armed only with a leather sling and five smooth stones. "You come against me with sword and spear and javelin," David told his enemy, "but I come against you in the name of the Lord Almighty, the God of the armies of Israel, whom you have defied. This day the Lord will deliver you into my hands, and I'll strike you down and cut off your head."

David killed Goliath with a single stone, and became a hero throughout Israel. King Saul made David a high-ranking officer in the army of Israel. When the Israelite army returned in triumph from battle, the people of Israel chanted, "Saul has slain his thousands, and

David his tens of thousands." From then on, Saul became jealous and fearful of David, and tried to murder him several times. Saul also tried to maneuver David into being killed in battle. Eventually, David had to flee for his life.

King Saul pursued David into the desert. In a compelling scene in 1 Samuel 24, David is hiding in a desert cave and King Saul enters the dark cave, unaware that David is close enough to slit his throat. David silently sneaks up on Saul and cuts a piece of fabric from Saul's robe. Saul leaves the cave and starts down the hillside—then David emerges from the cave and calls out to King Saul.

Saul whirls around and sees David standing in front of the cave, holding a piece of cloth over his head. "Look at this piece of your robe in my hand!" David says. "I cut off the corner of your robe but did not kill you.… May the Lord avenge the wrongs you have done to me, but my hand will not touch you."

Hearing David's words, Saul weeps in remorse. "You are more righteous than I," he says. "May the Lord reward you well for the way you treated me today. I know that you will surely be king and that the kingdom of Israel will be established in your hands. Now swear to me by the Lord that you will not kill off my descendants or wipe out my name from my father's family."

David gives his solemn promise to Saul—but he remains in his stronghold, knowing that Saul's word can't be trusted. And true enough, Saul eventually has second thoughts and again tries to hunt down and destroy David.

But Saul's reign ultimately comes to an end. In 1 Samuel 31, King Saul goes to war against the Philistines, and his three sons, including Jonathan, are killed in fierce fighting. Philistine archers wound Saul, and he begs his armor-bearer to run him through with a sword to prevent the Philistines from torturing him. When the armor-bearer refuses, Saul falls on his own sword and collapses, mortally wounded but still alive. An Amalekite later comes upon Saul and delivers the death-blow.

After David learns of Saul's death, he hears the voice of the Lord tell him to go to Hebron. David obeys. There, at about age thirty, David is publicly anointed King over Judah, the southern kingdom. Years later, when David is about thirty-seven, the elders of Israel go to King David at his capital in Hebron and anoint him King over the northern kingdom as well.

Israel and Judah become one nation under the competent leadership of King David. He leads the army of Israel to war against the Jebusites—a pagan tribe that even Joshua was unable to defeat during the conquest of Canaan. The arrogant Jebusites stand on the walls of Jebus, their fortress, mocking David and his army.

David knows that the fortress of the Jebusites is too strong to attack with a conventional assault. He sends several of his men to search for the secret water shaft that supplies the Jebusites with drinking water. Then he offers honor and promotion to the soldier who volunteers to enter the Jebusite stronghold via the water shaft and open the gates of the city.

A man named Joab, son of Zeruiah, locates the water shaft, which was connected to the Gihon Spring on the eastern slope of Mount Zion. Joab climbs up the shaft and opens the gates of the city so that David's army can enter and conquer the city. (The shaft that Joab entered was discovered in 1867 by British engineer Sir Charles Warren, and is now known as Warren's Shaft. Ceramics found in the tunnel have established that this shaft was in use when the Jebusites controlled the city.)

After David's army conquers the Jebusite fortress, the Israelites rename it "the City of David." The mountain on which the city was built is called Mount Zion, and nearby, to the north, is Mount Moriah. The Israelites give the Jebusite city a new name: Jerusalem. David moves the capital of Israel from Hebron to Jerusalem.

THE KING DAVID ADMINISTRATION

In Jerusalem, the Scriptures tell us, David administered justice, ruling the nation with discernment, fairness, and impartiality. He appointed qualified leaders to oversee various departments of his administration, and he exercised oversight to make sure that they acted fairly, vindicated the innocent, and punished wrongdoers.

In 1 Chronicles 27, we see that David reorganized the Israelite military into a national militia under the leadership of Joab (the man who climbed up the water shaft and opened the gates, giving Israel victory over the Jebusites). David's army was organized into twelve divisions, each division consisting of 24,000 men. Each division would be on duty for one month out of the year, so that all Israelite men capable of bearing arms took a month-long term in the military. This left each man with eleven months of the year to operate his farm or business.

The same passage, 1 Chronicles 27, shows how David organized the civil government and the economic activity of the kingdom. He placed overseers in charge of the royal storehouses, workers, vineyards, wineries, olive groves, oil presses, herds, flocks, and other property. He also had wise men who provided insight and counsel for important decisions.

David also elevated the role of the priesthood in the nation, and made the people more conscious of their need to serve and worship God. David himself composed many of the Psalms that were used in worship. Through his sacred artistry, David was able to instruct the nation and remind the people that they were to worship God alone, and have nothing to do with the idols and false gods of the pagan nations.

King David was a master delegator. He organized his government to make effective use of the genius and industriousness of all the Israelite people. He distributed authority to heroic warriors like Joab, Abishai, and Benaiah; to wise executives and counselors like Jehoshaphat, Sheva, Adoram, Ira the Jairite, Ahithophel, and Hushai; to trustworthy prophets like Nathan and Gad, and to dedicated priests and music ministers like Zadok, Abiathar, and Asaph.

In Psalm 78, Asaph recalled how God blessed His people by establishing David as King over the nation:

> He chose David his servant
>> and took him from the sheep pens;
> from tending the sheep he brought him
>> to be the shepherd of his people Jacob,
>> of Israel his inheritance.
> And David shepherded them with integrity of heart;
>> with skillful hands he led them. (Ps. 78:70-72 NIV)

In these lines, Asaph, King David's music and worship minister, writes about how God chose a young shepherd boy, and made him King over Israel. God took David from the sheep pens and placed him in the throne room, making him shepherd over the entire nation of Israel. God delights in taking lowly people out of obscurity, and using them in a mighty way.

Asaph goes on to say that King David shepherded the people "with integrity of heart, with skillful hands"—poetic language to describe both the compassionate wisdom ("integrity of heart") and the organizational competence ("skillful hands") of King David's administration. It's not enough for a leader to care for his people. A leader must also be competent to make the organization work efficiently and effectively for the good of the people. King David perfectly balanced compassion and competence in his administration.

Some leaders are long on compassion and short on competence. While they excel at empathizing and sympathizing with the problems of the people, they are incompetent at solving those problems. They are good shepherds but bad kings.

Other leaders are long on competence but short on compassion. Their government operates efficiently, but is out of touch with the real needs of the people. They are good kings but bad shepherds.

David, the Shepherd-King, perfectly combined compassion and competence in a leadership model that we all should emulate. He had "integrity of heart," a true heart, a compassionate heart, a shepherd's heart—and he had "skillful hands," organizational and administrative competence, the ability to make an organization function effectively.

Israel's greatest king was a foreshadow of the coming Messiah, the ultimate Shepherd-King. When Jesus returns to establish His Kingdom, He will rule with perfect compassion and absolute competence.

THE ROYAL PSALM

Psalm 72 is a psalm about the responsibilities of the king, and in most English translations, it carries the inscription, "Of Solomon," suggesting that King Solomon, the son of David, was the author. Yet the very last line of Psalm 72 reads, "This concludes the prayers of David son of Jesse." Some Bible scholars have suggested that this inscription means that David composed this psalm for his son Solomon. But I think there is a more likely explanation for this inscription.

I believe the author of Psalm 72 was Solomon, and that the psalm is based on a prayer that David spoke, perhaps in the closing days of his life. The words of the psalm read more like the Psalms of David then the writings of Solomon (such as Ecclesiastes or The Song of Solomon). I think Psalm 72 expresses the thoughts, emotions, and leadership principles of King David, as captured by the pen of his son, the future King Solomon. This psalm also gives us a glimpse into the future reign of Jesus when He returns and rules from the New Jerusalem. Here is the leadership vision of King David, as recorded in The Royal Psalm, Psalm 72:

Endow the king with your justice, O God,
> the royal son with your righteousness.
May he judge your people in righteousness,
> your afflicted ones with justice.

May the mountains bring prosperity to the people,
> the hills the fruit of righteousness.
May he defend the afflicted among the people
> and save the children of the needy;
> may he crush the oppressor.
May he endure as long as the sun,
> as long as the moon, through all generations.
May he be like rain falling on a mown field,
> like showers watering the earth.
In his days may the righteous flourish
> and prosperity abound till the moon is no more.

May he rule from sea to sea
> and from the River to the ends of the earth.
May the desert tribes bow before him
> and his enemies lick the dust.

May the kings of Tarshish and of distant shores
    bring tribute to him.
May the kings of Sheba and Seba
    present him gifts.
May all kings bow down to him
    and all nations serve him.

For he will deliver the needy who cry out,
    the afflicted who have no one to help.
He will take pity on the weak and the needy
    and save the needy from death.
He will rescue them from oppression and violence,
    for precious is their blood in his sight.

Long may he live!
    May gold from Sheba be given him.
May people ever pray for him
    and bless him all day long.
May grain abound throughout the land;
    on the tops of the hills may it sway.
May the crops flourish like Lebanon
    and thrive like the grass of the field.
May his name endure forever;
    may it continue as long as the sun.

Then all nations will be blessed through him,
    and they will call him blessed.

Praise be to the Lord God, the God of Israel,
    who alone does marvelous deeds.
Praise be to his glorious name forever;
    may the whole earth be filled with his glory.

Amen and Amen.

This concludes the prayers of David son of Jesse.

In this prayerful psalm, David lays out the key responsibilities of a leader—to administer justice, to lead with righteousness, to judge with impartiality, to defend the defenseless and afflicted, to promote prosperity among the people, to save the children of the needy, and to punish oppressors. David also pronounces a blessing on the godly leader—that he might endure and live a long life, that his influence would spread to the ends of the earth, that his enemies would fear him, and that his people would flourish and prosper. David also expressed a prayer that the righteous leader's name would endure, that all nations would be blessed because of him, and that God would be praised and glorified because of his godly leadership.

That prayer should be our prayer as we live out our leadership lives. This prayer of King David, this psalm of King Solomon, is a vision of how every godly leader should lead. These goals should be our goals, these responsibilities should be our responsibilities, so that we would glorify God through our leadership, whether we lead a family, a church, a corporation, or a government.

LESSONS IN COMPETENT LEADERSHIP

The Books of 1 Kings and 1 Chronicles record parallel accounts of the death of King David: "Then David rested with his ancestors and was buried in the City of David. He had reigned forty years over Israel—seven years in Hebron and thirty-three in Jerusalem" (1 Kings 2:10-11 NIV). "David son of Jesse was king over all Israel. He ruled over Israel forty years—seven in Hebron and thirty-three in Jerusalem. He died at a good old age, having enjoyed long life, wealth and honor. His son Solomon succeeded him as king" (1 Chron. 29:26-28 NIV).

King David served in a number of leadership roles during his reign: Warrior. Poet. Worship leader. Legislator. Judge. Administrator. David lived about a thousand years before Christ, and his reign was Israel's golden age. David's son Solomon expanded the wealth, power, borders, and influence of Israel even beyond what King David achieved, but it was David who united two poor, small tribal domains into an empire. Solomon merely built upon the empire his father David established.

The nation King David inherited from King Saul was a fractured commonwealth of thirteen struggling, squabbling tribes—tribes that were weak and oppressed by the Philistines, Amalekites, and other hostile pagan nations. King David battled the godless nations into submission, transforming Israel into the sole superpower of the region. The Scriptures tell us, "In everything he [David] did he had great success, because the Lord was with him" (1 Sam. 18:14 NIV).

After King David subdued the Philistines on Israel's western border, he successfully attacked the Jebusites and seized control of Jerusalem—his new capital city. He brought the Ark of the Covenant to Jerusalem, and the worship of God became the chief unifying force in the nation, welding Israel and Judah together as "one nation under God." Next, David turned his attention to Israel's troubled eastern border, defeating the Moabites and the Ammonites. This not only brought peace to the region, but those nations became vassal states, and poured tribute into the treasury of Israel. With peace came increased trade—and Israel's dominance over international trade routes transformed Israel into an economic powerhouse.

Under the Jebusites, Jerusalem had been an important city-state in Canaan, strong and defiant behind its walls, but geographically confined to a few square miles. Under King David, Jerusalem became a city of wealth, power, and splendor. No longer merely a tribal fortress, Jerusalem became an internationally famed seat of power and center of worship and culture for the growing Jewish empire.

The increasing wealth of the nation of Israel demanded that King David be an able and competent administrator. Wealth poured into the nation in the form of tribute from vassal kings, the spoils of various wars, and taxes collected from outlying provinces. Crops, orchards, herds, and flocks brought still more wealth into the royal treasury. All this wealth enabled King David to lay plans for the construction of a new Temple in Jerusalem. David himself would not live to see the Temple built, but David's administration generated the wealth that would finance the construction of the many-splendored Temple of Solomon.

King David was a leader whose competence we should all emulate. What are the leadership lessons of David's life?

FIRST LESSON: *To become a competent leader, you've got to pay your dues.*

King David was one of the most amazingly capable and competent leaders in history. How did he become such a brilliantly competent leader? Answer: David paid his dues. When did he pay his dues? When did he undergo the mentoring and training he needed to become competent as a leader? It took place in the long span of time between his first anointing and his second anointing.

The first anointing of David was a private ceremony, conducted by the prophet Samuel, involving only David, his father Jesse, his brothers, and possibly a few elders of the town of Bethlehem. David was only seventeen at the time. The second anointing of David was a public ceremony in Hebron, then the capital of Judah. David was about thirty at the time.

In the thirteen or fourteen years between the first and second anointing, David lived in obscurity. He spent some of his time minding his father's flocks in the wilderness. He also served an apprenticeship in the court of King Saul as a poet, musician, and squire to the King. He was the closest friend to Jonathan the Prince. He probably talked to the top military leaders and diplomats of Israel. He studied warfare and statesmanship.

Before God could elevate him to the throne of Israel, David had to study statesmanship, diplomacy, and war strategy to prove himself competent to lead. He learned still more about leadership as an exiled warlord, the leader of a band of outlaws being pursued by King Saul. He became a legendary folk hero among the people, and after the death of King Saul, the people readily acclaimed David as their king. David's life exemplifies the principle that those who would lead must undergo training and mentoring so they will be ready when their moment comes.

SECOND LESSON: *Great leaders should strive to be complete, not just competent.*

There's a tragic note to King David's story. Though he was a skilled and competent leader, and a man after God's own heart, he had a flaw in his character that he failed to deal with. Though David possessed an abundance of the Fifth Side of Leadership: Competence, he had a gap in his armor regarding the Fourth Side of Leadership: Character. King David had a roving eye, and when he began to lust after Bathsheba, the wife of one of his soldiers, he started down a road that led to adultery and murder.

In 2 Samuel 11:1, we see where King David made his first mistake: "In the spring, at the time when kings go off to war, David sent Joab out with the king's men and the whole Israelite army. They destroyed the Ammonites and besieged Rabbah. But David remained in Jerusalem." Springtime was the time when kings made war and either extended or defended their boundaries. David should have been with his soldiers, defending the nation. Instead, he remained in Jerusalem. He neglected his duties.

While walking on the roof of his palace, he saw a beautiful woman named Bathsheba as she was taking a bath. He desired her, and made up his mind to have an affair with her. He seduced her— and she became pregnant. To cover up his sin, he tried to persuade her husband, Uriah, to spend time with Bathsheba and have relations with her. But Uriah was more faithful to his duty then David was, and he refused to be with his wife while his men were on the battlefield.

Finally, David arranged for some of his soldiers to betray Uriah and leave him unprotected to be killed by the enemy. This story shows how low a man of God can sink once he yields himself to sin and lies. Though Uriah was killed by the Ammonites, it was as if David murdered Uriah with his own hands. King David had become an adulterer and a murderer, and he might have ended up like King Saul, haunted by guilt and suspicion, bereft of God's Spirit—but God in His mercy sent the prophet Nathan to confront King David and shame him into confessing and repenting of his sin.

We need all Seven Sides of Leadership working together to make us complete as leaders. The Fourth Side, Character, is vitally important to leadership, as King David discovered to his lasting regret. He was a great ruler, an effective administrator, a just and incorruptible judge, and a man who served God with a passion bordering on fanaticism—but he was incomplete as a leader because he failed to maintain the absolute integrity of his character.

THIRD LESSON: *Great leaders should be polymaths.*

What, you may ask, is a polymath? It's a person with expertise in many different subjects. King David was a farm boy at heart. He had been raised and instructed by his father Jesse to manage the family ranch near Bethlehem. David probably learned more than simply how to tend sheep. His father Jesse probably taught him the principles of agrarian economics and farm management, and how to raise wheat, wine grapes, and other crops for a profit.

David also learned how to compose music, write poetry, and accompany himself on a stringed instrument, the lyre. During his apprenticeship to King Saul, he learned the art of statesmanship, the art of war, and the art of diplomacy. He probably studied history and literature as well. The ability to demonstrate competence in a variety of fields enables a leader to draw upon interdisciplinary knowledge. It has been said that, to the man with a hammer, every problem is a nail. But if you have a large and varied toolbox of knowledge, experience, and training, you'll be better equipped to solve the problems that a hammer can't fix.

The broader and deeper your understanding of the wide variety of subjects, the more competent a leader you will be. To be a great leader, be a reader, a lifelong learner, and a polymath.

FOURTH LESSON: *Competent leaders must be courageous.*
David faced many daunting challenges, both in his early life and in his leadership life. As a boy, he battled—and overcame—a lion, a bear, and a gigantic Philistine warrior. By facing and overcoming these challenges, David ratcheted up his courage and his confidence to face greater challenges down the road. When he faced Goliath, armed only with a leather sling and five smooth stones, he had confidence in God and confidence in his own skill with a slingshot.

If a leader lacks courage, if a leader lacks confidence, all the competence in the world won't help. As a basketball player, you might have the skill and competence to shoot 500 three-pointers in a row in practice—but if your hands shake and your knees wobble in the big game, what good is all that skill? You must have the courage and confidence to make the shot when the pressure is on. As a leader, that means you need the confidence and courage to make high-quality decisions, instantly and under pressure—you can't freeze or fold when the chips are down. David's courage and confidence enabled him to demonstrate his leadership competence in clutch situations.

Very few people are born with confidence and courage. You acquire these qualities by accepting increasingly more difficult challenges over time. As you take on a tough challenge—and accomplish it—you grow your confidence for the next challenge. The story of David's life is the story of a young man who overcame a series of obstacles and challenges, each one more difficult than the one before. To increase your competence and grow your confidence, pattern your life after his. Seek out new challenges and new ways of testing yourself. Trust God; leap out of your comfort zone, and you'll be amazed at how courageous you are.

FIFTH LESSON: *Competent leaders are immune to criticism.*
Every leader gets criticized. It comes with the territory. Some criticism is valid—so learn from it and keep going. But some criticism comes from misunderstanding, jealousy, or just plain spite—so ignore it and keep going.

Late in King David's life, he suffered a major setback. His son Absalom usurped the throne of Israel. David was forced to flee into exile. In 2 Samuel 16, we see David and his men on the run. One of David's sworn enemies, Shimei of the clan of Saul, cursed David as he and his men were on the road to Bahurim. Shimei threw stones at David and his soldiers, shouting, "Get out, get out, you murderer, you scoundrel! The Lord has repaid you for all the blood you shed in the household of Saul, in whose place you have reigned. The Lord has given the kingdom into the hands of your son Absalom. You have come to ruin because you are a murderer!"

One of David's men said, "Why should this dead dog curse my lord the king? Let me go over and cut off his head!"

But King David wouldn't allow it. He said, "If he is cursing because the Lord said to him, 'Curse David,' who can ask, 'Why do you do this?' ... Leave him alone; let him curse, for the Lord has told him to. It may be that the Lord will look upon my misery and restore me to His covenant blessing instead of His curse today."

David acknowledged that he had sinned, and he suspected that he was suffering the consequences of his sin. His own son had removed him from the throne, and now this relative of Saul's was tormenting him with curses and stones. David chose to ignore this man's curses. He trusted God to be just, and hoped God would see how he endured suffering without complaint or retaliation.

There is a powerful leadership lesson for you and me in David's response to Shimei. As leaders, we need the hide of a rhinoceros. Our opponents, and sometimes even our friends, will criticize us, curse us, and cast stones at us. Sometimes we have it coming. Sometimes we don't. But God will look upon us favorably if we absorb criticism without complaining or retaliating. Don't give in to anger, hate, or self-pity. Become immune to criticism. That's what King David did. That's what competent leaders do.

COMPETENT AND DECISIVE

John C. Maxwell once said, "Competence goes beyond words. It's the leader's ability to say it, plan it, and do it in such a way that others know that you know how—and know that they want to follow you." One leader who exemplified those words was General Dwight David

Eisenhower. Not only was David his middle name, but he was a competent leader in the King David mold.

Dwight Eisenhower was raised in a Mennonite family in Kansas, and if you know anything about Mennonites, you know they are a devoutly pacifist Christian sect. Dwight Eisenhower and his five brothers were taught never to get into fights with other children in the neighborhood or at school. Dwight's father David came home from work one day to see a neighborhood boy chasing young Dwight down the street. David called his son over and said, "Why do you let that boy chase you around like that?"

Dwight said, "If I fight him, you'll give me a whipping whether I win or lose!"

David pointed at the boy, who was watching and sneering. "Ike," David said, using Dwight's nickname, "you chase that boy out of here!" And Ike did as his father said. The bully never chased him again.[25]

Dwight's father didn't raise his sons to start fights, but he didn't want his sons to be chased around or beaten up by other kids. He raised his sons to be competent and competitive, and to continually improve their leadership skills. Historian Stephen Ambrose explained:

In a family of six boys, competition was the natural order of things. Who could do the best job at this or that task? Who could run the fastest? Jump the highest? Lift the heaviest weight? Read the Bible aloud most accurately? Daily, in countless ways, the boys tested themselves against one another. David and Ida [Dwight's parents] encouraged this competition, encouraged them to be ambitious to do the best. Most of all, each of the boys wanted to be the toughest, and they fought among themselves to find out who was the best scrapper.[26]

Dwight's favorite subject in school was history—especially military history. In September 1910, he won an appointment to West Point—much to the dismay of his Mennonite parents. Yet both his mother and father were on hand to wish him well as he boarded the train for West Point.

During his early military career, Eisenhower impressed his superiors with his competence as a leader and administrator. As a commander of the tank training center at Camp Meade, Maryland, Eisenhower devised a new strategy of speed-oriented tank warfare. His ideas have been proven in combat, from World War II to Desert Storm.

Beginning in 1933, Eisenhower served as an aide to General Douglas MacArthur. He spent seven years with MacArthur, much of it in the Philippines. MacArthur wrote of Eisenhower in one fitness report, "This is the best officer in the Army. When the next war comes, he should go right to the top."[27] Despite that praise, MacArthur inexplicably kept Eisenhower from being promoted—perhaps because he viewed Eisenhower as a potential rival. Like King David, Eisenhower was patient. He served a long apprenticeship under General MacArthur.

Historian Matthew F. Holland observed that Eisenhower's apprenticeship to MacArthur—a general with a massive ego and a strong personality—probably helped prepare Eisenhower for his special role during World War II "when he had to work with such egotistical characters as Franklin D. Roosevelt, Winston Churchill, Charles de Gaulle, George S. Patton, and Bernard Montgomery."[28] (Those skills would later serve Eisenhower well in the White House.)

In 1941, Ike was appointed commander of the Third Army. Rising quickly, he was promoted to brigadier general by September of that year. After the attack on Pearl Harbor, Army Chief of Staff George Marshall appointed Eisenhower to the War Plans Division in

Washington, where he planned strategies for the Allied invasions of Europe and Japan.

In March 1942, Ike was named head of the Operations Division of the War Department and promoted to major general. In June, General Marshall sent Eisenhower to London as Commanding General, European Theater of Operations. Gen. Marshall had such confidence in Eisenhower's competence that he passed over 366 more senior officers to give Eisenhower the job.

In December 1943, President Roosevelt chose Eisenhower to be Supreme Allied Commander in Europe. This son of Mennonite pacifists was charged with planning and overseeing the liberation of Western Europe. To this day, Eisenhower's plan is considered the most complex and challenging military campaign in human history. It involved sending an Allied invasion force of 4,400 ships, 11,000 planes, and 155,000 assault troops across the English Channel in the hope of catching the enemy by surprise.

In the early hours of June 5, 1944, General Eisenhower and other senior members of the Allied High Command gathered in the map room of Southwick House in England. They studied intelligence and weather reports, and Eisenhower invited all opinions, but the decision was his alone. Ships of several nations steamed toward France, and the decision had to be made before it was too late to recall them.

After hearing all the information and opinions, Ike was silent for several moments. Then he said, "Okay, let's go."

He had prepared a note that read, "Our landings have failed and I have withdrawn our troops. If any blame or fault attaches to the attempt, it is mine alone."

Just after midnight, advance troops parachuted into France. As the sun rose, Allied landing craft and amphibious tanks reached the beaches. Allied troops waded into a hail of German artillery and machine gun fire. In the first hours of the invasion, ten thousand soldiers were killed or wounded—but the invasion succeeded. The Allies secured eighty square miles of French coastline—and General Eisenhower didn't need the note he had prepared.

The invasion was costly but successful. Under the competent leadership of General Eisenhower, the Allies began the task of liberating Europe. It had taken years of patient learning, acquiring skills, and gaining experience for Eisenhower to reach that level of leadership competence.

But like King David, Eisenhower paid his dues, mastered the art of war, and helped lead the world to peace. To be a complete leader, study the example of King David. Study the Fifth Side of Leadership: Competence.

CHAPTER 6: QUESTIONS FOR REFLECTION AND DISCUSSION

1. King David set an example of leadership competence. What qualities did he possess that set him apart as a competent leader? How did he acquire these qualities? How can you build these qualities into your own leadership life?

2. List two or three examples of the competence of King David. What do these examples say to you about the importance of competence to effective leadership? What lessons can you learn from the competent administration of King David?

   What insights do you see in the life of King David that you can apply to your own leadership life today? What steps can you take this week to become a more competent leader like King David?

3. In 1 Chronicles 27, we see how King David organized the civil government, the military, the economic sector, and the priesthood of the nation. He showed competent administrative ability in these different aspects of the life of the nation. You are probably a leader in one of these arenas—government, the military, the business sector, or the church. How does the administrative competence of King David help you better understand your role in your own leadership arena? Cite examples from your own experience.

4. King David was a master delegator who organized his government to make effective use of the genius of his people. One conclusion we can draw is that the most competent leaders of all are those who maximize the competence of their subordinates. What

lessons do you learn from King David about delegating as a facet of leadership competence?

5. Meditate in Psalm 72, the Royal Psalm, every day for a week. Write down the insights that God brings to your mind as you consider the insights of that psalm.

6. The life of King David teaches us that competent leaders don't let criticism get them down. We should learn from valid criticism and shrug off misplaced criticism. Do you let criticism roll off your back—or do your critics sometimes get in your head and diminish your effectiveness? What lessons do you learn from King David about responding to critics?

7. Young David served an internship in the court of King Saul. He observed King Saul going about his duties; he befriended and learned from the king's son, Jonathan; he had opportunities to question soldiers, diplomats, and bureaucrats in King Saul's government. Before Saul invited David to serve in the palace, David probably learned many lessons in economics, commerce, and management by assisting his father Jesse in operating a prosperous ranching and farming operation near Bethlehem.

    Have you ever been mentored or trained for leadership? How valuable was that mentoring or training in helping you become competent to lead?

    Have you ever mentored or trained young people to be leaders? What steps would you like to take this week to encourage young people to be leaders?

CHAPTER 7

MOSES:
BOLD LEADERSHIP

Dietrich Bonhoeffer was a pastor in Berlin during the rise of the Nazi Party in the 1930s. He was appalled by Hitler's message of hate, and even more horrified to see Nazi anti-Semitism infecting the German state church. In 1934, Bonhoeffer and other pastors founded the "Confessing Church" to oppose Nazism. Three years later, the Gestapo (the Nazi state police) imprisoned many of Bonhoeffer's seminary students and closed the seminary where he taught. Bonhoeffer continued to speak out.

In 1939, he left Germany to teach at an American seminary—but within days, he regretted the move. He told a friend, "I made a mistake in coming to America … I shall have no right to take part in the restoration of Christian life in Germany after the war unless I share the trials of this time with my people." He returned to Germany and joined the resistance.

As Hitler's war machine rumbled across Europe, Bonhoeffer joined Operation Seven, a group formed to help Jews escape to Switzerland. He also joined a plot to assassinate Hitler. This was a difficult decision, because Bonhoeffer had always been a pacifist. Yet he believed the death of Hitler could save millions of lives.

On July 20, 1944, Colonel Claus von Stauffenberg—who was secretly a member of the Resistance—left a suitcase bomb in Hitler's offices at Wolf's Lair fortress. The blast failed to kill Hitler, and Bonhoeffer's connection to the conspirators was discovered. The Gestapo sent him to Buchenwald, and later to the Flossenburg concentration camp. He was hanged on April 9, 1945, at the age of thirty-nine—just three weeks before the war ended. A German doctor witnessed the hanging and said that Bonhoeffer went to the gallows "brave and composed," adding, "I have hardly ever seen a man die so entirely submissive to the will of God."[29]

What finer, more fitting epitaph could anyone want? Dietrich Bonhoeffer was a bold leader. He was, in many ways, a lot like Moses.

LIBERATOR, LAWGIVER, AND LEADER

The Israelites had come into Egypt when Joseph was Pharaoh's chief advisor, the second most powerful man in Egypt. At that time, the contingent of Israelites living in Egypt consisted of Jacob (the father of the Israelite people), Jacob's twelve sons, and their wives and children—seventy people in all. Exodus 1 tells us that, generation by generation, "they multiplied greatly."

Joseph and his family members were welcomed into Egyptian society because of Pharaoh's gratitude to Joseph for guiding the nation through a time of famine. Jacob's descendants became prosperous and numerous in the land of Egypt. But after four centuries rolled by, the situation abruptly changed:

> Then a new king, to whom Joseph meant nothing, came to power in Egypt. "Look," he said to his people, "the Israelites have become far too numerous for us. Come, we must deal shrewdly with them or they will become even more numerous and, if war breaks out, will join our enemies, fight against us and leave the country."

So they put slave masters over them to oppress them with forced labor … (Exod. 1:8-11a NIV)

Fearing the growing numbers of the Hebrews, Pharaoh ordered all the male Hebrew children be drowned in the Nile. During this crisis, Moses was born to a woman named Jochebed. Jochebed placed baby Moses in a basket of woven papyrus and hid the child among the reeds by the riverbank. She placed Miriam, the sister of Moses, nearby to keep an eye on him.

The daughter of Pharaoh went to the river, found the basket, and realized it was one of the Hebrew babies. Miriam approached the Egyptian princess and offered to get one of the Hebrew women to nurse the baby. So Miriam went and got her mother and the Egyptian princess paid Jochebed to nurse her own baby. After Moses was weaned, Pharaoh's daughter adopted him and raised him in the palace as her own son.

Moses grew up as an Egyptian, yet he knew he was born a Hebrew. One day he saw an Egyptian overseer beating one of the Hebrew slaves. Moses killed the Egyptian and hid the dead man's body in the sand.

The following day, Moses went out again and saw two Hebrews fighting. He broke up the fight and said, "Why are you hitting each other?" One of the men replied, "Who made you ruler and judge over us? Are you thinking of killing me as you killed the Egyptian?"

Moses had thought there were no witnesses to the killing of the Egyptian, but these two Hebrews knew what he had done. How many others knew? Fearing Pharaoh's death penalty, Moses fled to the land of Midian (in what is today northwestern Saudi Arabia), and took refuge at the home of a Midianite priest named Jethro (also called Reuel). Moses married one of Jethro's daughters, and she gave birth to a son.

Meanwhile in Egypt, the Pharaoh died, but the suffering of the Israelite people continued.

On Mount Horeb, "the mountain of God" (which many Bible scholars believe is another name for Mount Sinai), God spoke to Moses from a burning bush. God instructed Moses to return to Egypt and to lead the Israelites out of bondage and into the land of Canaan, the promised land. "I will be with you," God said. "And this will be the sign to you that it is I who have sent you: When you have brought the people out of Egypt, you will worship God on this mountain."

Moses said, "Suppose I go to the Israelites and say to them, 'The God of your fathers has sent me to you,' and they ask me, 'What is his name?' Then what shall I tell them?"

"I AM WHO I AM," God said. "This is what you are to say to the Israelites: 'I AM has sent me to you.'"

Moses went back to Egypt to carry out God's command. Moses contended with Pharaoh in a series of confrontations, and finally, after God sent a series of ten plagues, Pharaoh agreed to let the Israelites leave Egypt. Common sense would have led Moses to take his people by the shortest, most direct route, the road north through Philistine country. But God told Moses that if the people encountered opposition from the Philistines, they might lose heart and return to Egypt. So Moses led the people by the longer road across the desert toward the Red Sea.

Along the way, God told Moses, "I will harden Pharaoh's heart, and he will pursue them. But I will gain glory for myself through Pharaoh and all his army, and the Egyptians will know that I am the Lord" (Exod. 14:4 NIV). Just as God said, Pharaoh changed his mind and sent his army to pursue the Israelites.

When the Israelites saw the army of Pharaoh coming after them, they lost their nerve. Some berated Moses, "Didn't we say to you in Egypt, 'Leave us alone; let us serve the Egyptians'? It would have been better for us to serve the Egyptians than to die in the desert!" (Exod. 14:11b-12 NIV).

In an amazing display of bold faith and courageous leadership, Moses said to the people, "Do not be afraid. Stand firm and you will see the deliverance the Lord will bring you today. The Egyptians you see today you will never see again. The Lord will fight for you; you need only to be still" (Exod. 14:13b-14 NIV).

Then Moses, in obedience to God, raised his staff toward the sea. The Scriptures tell us that "all that night the Lord drove the sea back with a strong east wind and turned it into dry land. The waters were divided, and the Israelites went through the sea on dry ground, with a wall of water on their right and on their left" (Exod. 14:21b-22 NIV). The Egyptians pursued the Israelites, the waters returned to their original place, and the entire army of Pharaoh perished. The Israelites were free and safe on the other side.

Moses led the Israelites to Mount Sinai, where God gave him the Ten Commandments, inscribed on stone tablets. While Moses was on the mountain, the people made an idol, the statue of a golden calf, and they worshiped it. When Moses returned and saw the idolatry of his people, he was overcome with anger, broke the tablets, and punished the people for their idolatry. He wrote down the Commandments on new tablets and commanded the people to make a covenant with God that they would be His people, He would be their God, and they would obey His commandments.

From Mount Sinai, Moses led his people to the Desert of Paran, on the western edge of the Arabian Peninsula. From there, Moses sent twelve spies North into Canaan, and they returned with proof of the richness of the land—but the spies also claimed the inhabitants were giant warriors who could not be defeated in battle. Only two of the spies, Joshua and Caleb, urged the Israelites to go boldly into Canaan and possess the promised land.

But the Israelites wanted to turn back. Some rebelled against Moses—and against God. Moses told the Israelites they were unworthy to inherit the promised land, and they would wander in the wilderness for forty years. Once this faithless generation had died out, their children would be allowed to possess the land. As Moses prophesied, the people wandered for forty years.

Moses led the people to the Jordan River. Across the river lay the promised land. Moses called the tribes together and reminded them that they could only be blessed by God if they lived according to His commandments. He sang a song of praise and blessed the people, then he appointed his successor, Joshua—one of the two bold and faithful spies who had believed God's promise. Joshua was also personally mentored and trained for leadership by Moses himself.

Finally, Moses climbed Mount Nebo and looked over the promised land. God let him see it, but God would not let him enter the land. There, on the mountaintop, Moses died. He was a hundred and twenty years old.

Moses was the liberator, lawgiver, and leader of Israel. He led his people out of slavery in the land of Egypt and received the Law from God on Mount Sinai. He appointed a bold young man as his successor. He is an excellent role model of bold leadership for you and me.

LIVING THE ADVENTURE OF BOLD LEADERSHIP

Moses began his leadership journey with reluctance and a deep sense of inadequacy. God transformed him into paragon of bold leadership—

a leader who dared to challenge the Egyptian Pharaoh, who dared to follow God to a seeming "dead end" at the Red Sea, who dared to climb a mountain to meet God face-to-face. He boldly confronted the sin and idolatry of his rebellious people, and he boldly led them to the doorstep of the promised land.

Knowing that the people would need bold leadership after he passed on, Moses selected Joshua as his successor. Moses mentored this energetic young man, teaching him to trust God and to dare great things for Him. In the opening lines of the Book of Joshua, we see that Moses chose well—and he prepared Joshua well for the leadership adventure that lay ahead of him:

> After the death of Moses the servant of the Lord, the Lord said to Joshua son of Nun, Moses' aide: "Moses my servant is dead. Now then, you and all these people, get ready to cross the Jordan River into the land I am about to give to them—to the Israelites. I will give you every place where you set your foot, as I promised Moses. Your territory will extend from the desert to Lebanon, and from the great river, the Euphrates—all the Hittite country—to the Mediterranean Sea in the west. No one will be able to stand against you all the days of your life. As I was with Moses, so I will be with you; I will never leave you nor forsake you. Be strong and courageous, because you will lead these people to inherit the land I swore to their ancestors to give them.
>
> Be strong and very courageous. Be careful to obey all the law my servant Moses gave you; do not turn from it to the right or to the left, that you may be successful wherever you go. Keep this Book of the Law always on your lips; meditate on it day and night, so that you may be careful to do everything

written in it. Then you will be prosperous and successful. Have I not commanded you? Be strong and courageous. Do not be afraid; do not be discouraged, for the Lord your God will be with you wherever you go. (Josh. 1:1-9 NIV)

And the Book of Joshua is the story of the bold leadership of the protégé and successor of Moses, Joshua. The key lesson we see in the lives of biblical leaders like Moses and Joshua is that if you're not bold, you are not a leader. An authentic leader can't afford to play it safe. As former Florida State football coach Bobby Bowden has said, "The Bible teaches us to 'fear not.' That's a good starting point for any aspiring leader." And the apostle Paul wrote to young Timothy, "For the Spirit God gave us does not make us timid, but gives us power, love and self-discipline" (2 Tim. 1:7 NIV).

Moses has symbolized bold leadership for all those who have suffered oppression and yearn for liberation. Moses was a symbol of hope for the leaders of the abolition movement during the era of slavery. When Abraham Lincoln was assassinated in 1865 after freeing the slaves, many African-Americans believed they had lost their Moses. Historian Charles Carleton Coffin described the parallels between these two bold leaders, Moses and Lincoln:

The millions whom Abraham Lincoln delivered from slavery will ever liken him to Moses, the deliverer of Israel.... One discovers God in the mystery of the burning bush at Horeb; to the other, in a restful retreat, comes the uplifting revelation that God is his Father, and all men his brothers. Moses gives just and righteous laws to Israel, Abraham Lincoln a new charter of liberty to his country. Both lead their fellow-men out of bondage, both behold the promised land of the nation's larger life, but neither is privileged to enter it.[30]

Dr. Martin Luther King, Jr., frequently talked about Moses in his sermons. On April 7, 1957, he opened and closed his message with references to the bold leadership of Moses. He said:

I want to preach this morning from the subject, "The Birth of a New Nation." And I would like to use as a basis for our thinking together a story that has long since been stenciled on the mental sheets of succeeding generations. It is the story of the Exodus, the story of the flight of the Hebrew people from the bondage of Egypt, through the wilderness, and finally to the promised land. It's a beautiful story.

I had the privilege the other night of seeing the story in movie terms in New York City, entitled *The Ten Command-ments*, and I came to see it in all its beauty—the struggle of Moses, the struggle of his devoted followers as they sought to get out of Egypt. And they finally moved on to the wil-derness and toward the promised land. This is something of the story of every people struggling for freedom....

Moses might not get to see Canaan, but his children will see it. He even got to the mountaintop enough to see it and that assured him that it was coming. But the beauty of the thing is that there's always a Joshua to take up his work and take the children on in. And it's there waiting with its milk and honey, and with all of the bountiful beauty that God has in store for His children. Oh, what exceedingly marvelous things God has in store for us. Grant that we will follow Him enough to gain them.[31]

Like Moses, Dr. King didn't live to see the promised land. He looked across the Jordan from his own mountaintop—then he was taken from us by an assassin's bullet. But he lived courageously, led boldly, and he changed the world.

LESSONS IN BOLD LEADERSHIP FROM THE LIFE OF MOSES

Down through the centuries, Moses has been an inspiration and a role model for generations of bold leaders. He continues to inspire you and me today. Here are some of the lessons we can learn from his courageous leadership life:

FIRST LESSON: *Bold leadership is consistent and principled: your walk must match your talk.*

This is a lesson Moses himself had to learn—the hard way. As a young man, living in the palace of Pharaoh, Moses saw an Egyptian beating a Hebrew slave. The impetuous young Moses decided to take the law into his own hands. He killed the Egyptian, hid the body, and thought no one would know what he had done. But there was a witness. Moses didn't know who had seen him commit the murder, but there was a witness—and the witness had spread the word of his crime.

Later, when Moses tried to assert his leadership and break up a fight between two Israelites, the men sneered at him. "Who made you ruler and judge over us?" one of them said. "Are you thinking of killing me as you killed the Egyptian?" By acting immorally and unlawfully, Moses had undermined his own credibility. The people looked at Moses and they didn't see a leader—they saw a murderer.

As a leader, your actions and your words must be consistent at all times. Your walk must match your talk. A leader who behaves in an unprincipled, immoral, or unlawful way undermines his or her own leadership. That was a painful leadership lesson Moses learned at an early age.

SECOND LESSON: *Bold leaders overcome self-doubt by letting go of delusions of self-sufficiency.*

Bold leaders trust in God, not in themselves. In Exodus 3, when Moses stood before the burning bush, he said to God, "Who am I that I should go to Pharaoh and bring the Israelites out of Egypt?"

Moses had every right to feel inadequate for the mission God gave him. He *was* inadequate. We are *all* inadequate, but God still wants to use us. God didn't want Moses to stand before Pharaoh in his own strength. God wanted to use Moses as an empty vessel that God Himself would fill with supernatural power and divinely chosen words. God chooses people for leadership—and he chooses people more often because of their weakness than because of their strength. This principle was never truer than in the life of Moses.

We see this principle again in Exodus chapters 5 and 6. Moses obeys God and goes to Pharaoh and demands, in God's name, that Pharaoh let the Israelites leave Egypt in peace. Pharaoh not only refuses, but he increases the workload of the Hebrew slaves. The Israelites blame Moses for increasing their sufferings.

So God again tells Moses, "Go, tell Pharaoh king of Egypt to let the Israelites go out of his country."

And Moses replies, "If the Israelites will not listen to me, why would Pharaoh listen to me, since I speak with faltering lips?"

Moses knows that his speech is clumsy. He knows he is inadequate for the task God has given him. He knows that he lacks the human skills and abilities to be a great leader. And that is exactly what God wants Moses to understand.

The apostle Paul knew how Moses must have felt. He struggled with a physical impediment he called a "thorn in the flesh." This impediment prevented Paul from being the kind of forceful, dynamic leader he wanted to be. Three times, Paul set aside special times of praying and fasting, imploring God to take away the "thorn in the flesh." Paul described God's answer in 2 Corinthians 12:9—"But he said to me, 'My grace is sufficient for you, for my power is made perfect in weakness.' Therefore I will boast all the more gladly about my weaknesses, so that Christ's power may rest on me."

Like Paul, Moses needed to accept his own inadequacy. He needed to let go of his delusions of self-sufficiency and accept the fact that he was a clumsy speaker and an unimpressive leader. He needed to accept it that even his own people didn't want to listen to him. The Israelites would be liberated by God's power—not by his eloquence or leadership skills. He needed to rely on God, not himself.

Once Moses was able to say, "I speak with faltering lips," God was able to use him. Once he had let go of his own delusion of self-sufficiency, he was able to cast himself on God's all-sufficient power.

THIRD LESSON: *Bold leaders trust God—but they keep moving.* They don't practice a static, sit-and-wait faith. They practice faith in motion. They translate their faith into meaningful kinetic action. They don't merely respond to change; they make change happen. Once again, this is a lesson Moses had to learn from God.

In Exodus 14, Moses and his people are sandwiched between the onrushing Egyptian army and the Red Sea. If God does not miraculously intervene, they are done for. At this point, the people panic and cry out to Moses, "Why did you bring us out into the desert to die?"

Moses tells the people, "Do not be afraid. Stand firm and you will see the deliverance the Lord will bring you today. The Egyptians you see today you will never see again. The Lord will fight for you; you need only to be still." Moses had great faith that God was going to rescue them, so he told the people to sit and wait for God's deliverance.

But that was not God's plan. The Lord said to Moses, "Why are you crying out to me? Tell the Israelites to move on."

In other words, don't sit and wait for God to deliver you. Yes, His power is on the way. His deliverance is coming. But you need to do your part. You need to take action and get moving. Don't practice a static, passive faith. Demonstrate a dynamic, active faith. Be a bold leader who sets your people in motion.

FOURTH LESSON: *Bold leadership inspires confident, trusting followership by achieving positive results.*

After the miraculous rescue at the Red Sea, the Israelites were ready to follow Moses anywhere. They had faith in God and confidence in the leader God had appointed, Moses the Liberator. When good things happen in your organization as a result of your bold and effective leadership, your people will follow you anywhere.

The key to achieving positive results is to start with God. Instead of asking Him to bless your ambitions, ask God to reveal His plan to you, then seek to align all of your plans and goals with His. Once you are convinced you're following the will of God, communicate your God-given vision to your people with confidence and assurance. As you make plans for your new leadership adventure, make sure you take into account contingencies and setbacks. Have a Plan B, Plan C, and Plan D ready—just in case.

Bold leaders are willing to take risks—but only calculated risks, not foolhardy gambles. If you seek God's will, then dare greatly, plan carefully, respond quickly to changing conditions, remain flexible, and lead confidently, chances are you'll achieve the kind of success that will inspire enthusiasm and trust among your followers.

FIFTH LESSON: *Bold leaders must be patient with timid and imperfect people.*

Patience doesn't always come naturally to leaders. When people demonstrate fear, reluctance, or complaining, we may feel tempted to lose patience with them.

In Exodus 15, as Moses led the people of Israel away from the Red Sea and into the desert of Shur, they began to worry about their water supply. They walked for three days without finding water. Finally, they came to the oasis of Marah (which means "bitter"), and they found the water at that oasis too bitter to drink. At that point, the same people who had cheered Moses as a hero after the miracle at the Red Sea now turned against him. They demanded to know, "What are we to drink?"

Now, it wasn't Moses's fault that the oasis had bitter water. His throat was as parched as theirs. But Moses was their leader, he was on the hot seat, and when things went wrong, the people blamed him. Moses didn't become impatient with them. He didn't shout at them, "What do you people want from me? I'm as thirsty as you are!" No, he absorbed their complaints, because that's what leaders do. Then he proceeded to consult with God, and he found a solution to the problem.

The Lord showed Moses a piece of wood, and told him to put it in the water of the bitter spring. Moses did so, and the water became sweet to drink. The people drank their fill, and then they moved on. Soon, they came to a lush oasis called Elim, where there were twelve springs and seventy palm trees. And the people camped beside the waters.

A leader cannot control every circumstance. A leader is not always responsible for problems and setbacks that arise. But a leader should always respond patiently to followers and their complaints. A bold leader must be a patient listener.

SIXTH LESSON: *Bold leadership does not mean going it alone.*
Never mistake bold leadership for rugged individualism. Bold leaders need wise counselors and advisors. Leaders who are bold to the point of being impulsive need a few wise counselors to keep them from taking boldness too far. Some leaders need counselors to help them keep their egos in check. And some leaders need advisors to remind them that leadership is delegating.

In Exodus 18, Jethro, the father-in-law of Moses, hears the news about the miraculous parting of the Red Sea. He rushes out to the desert where Moses and his people are camped. Moses and Jethro embrace, and Moses tells his father-in-law about everything the Lord has done. Jethro is overjoyed and praises God for rescuing the Israelites from the Egyptians. "Now I know that the Lord is greater than all other gods," Jethro says, "for he did this to those who had treated Israel arrogantly" (Exod. 18:11 NIV).

The next day, Moses takes his usual place as the judge for the people. Anyone who has a problem or dispute can come to Moses for a solution. The people stand around him from morning until evening, and Jethro watches this taking place. Finally, Jethro says to Moses, "What is this you are doing for the people? Why do you alone sit as judge, while all these people stand around you from morning till evening?"

Moses replies, "Because the people come to me to seek God's will. Whenever they have a dispute, it is brought to me, and I decide between the parties and inform them of God's decrees and instructions."

"What you are doing is not good," Jethro says. "You and these people who come to you will only wear yourselves out. The work is too heavy for you; you cannot handle it alone. Listen now to me and I will give you some advice, and may God be with you. You must be the people's representative before God and bring their disputes to him. Teach them his decrees and instructions, and show them the way they are to live and how they are to behave. But select capable men from all the people—men who fear God, trustworthy men who hate dishonest gain—and appoint them as officials over thousands, hundreds, fifties and tens. Have them serve as judges for the people at all times, but have them bring every difficult case to you; the simple cases they can decide themselves. That will make your load lighter, because they will share it with you. If you do this and God so commands, you will be able to stand the strain, and all these people will go home satisfied" (Exod. 18:13-23 NIV).

Moses is humble enough to receive and act upon Jethro's advice. Verse 24 tells us, "Moses listened to his father-in-law and did everything he said." Leaders need a few close relationships with trustworthy counselors—people who can be trusted with the leader's deepest fears and darkest secrets, people who have a close and daily walk with God, people with proven godly wisdom, people who aren't afraid to tell a leader what he or she needs to hear. Jethro was that kind of advisor to Moses.

Who is your "Jethro"? Who can you trust to give you wise counsel, to guard your confidences, to give you the truth straight from the shoulder? If you don't have a "Jethro," you should recruit one—or two or three—right away. Seek out the wisest people in your church or business or circle of friends. Meet with them on a regular basis. Seek their counsel when you face a tough decision.

Leaders also need close friends to support them in times of crisis. In Exodus 17, the Israelites encounter their first test on the battlefield. They are attacked by nomadic warriors, the Amalekites, at a place called Rephidim. The Israelites repel the raiders, but Moses knows they will be back if God's people don't seize the initiative.

Moses tells Joshua, "Choose some of our men and go out to fight the Amalekites. Tomorrow I will stand on top of the hill with the staff of God in my hands."

So Joshua takes the battle to the Amalekites while Moses, Aaron, and a man named Hur stand atop a hill to watch the battle. As long as Moses holds his hands up, Israel prevails over the enemy. But when Moses grows weary and lowers his arms, the momentum of battle turns against Israel. Aaron and Hur come alongside Moses and lift his arms, supporting Moses until the Israelites have defeated the Amalekites.

Leaders need people to support them when they feel weary, spent, and alone. Leaders can't do it all in their own strength. Who is your Aaron? Who is your Hur? Who lifts your arms when you grow weary of the battle? Bold leaders don't try to do it all themselves. Bold leaders don't pretend to have all the answers. Bold leaders don't hide their fears, doubts, and weaknesses from close friends and supporters. Moses needed advice and strength from others—and so do we.

SEVENTH LESSON: *Bold leaders continually teach, preach, and exemplify faithfulness to God.*

Throughout the books of Moses, we see Moses commanding the people to seek God's will and obey God's laws. In Deuteronomy 4, Moses tells the people:

> Now, Israel, hear the decrees and laws I am about to teach you. Follow them so that you may live and may go in and take possession of the land the Lord, the God of your ancestors, is giving you. Do not add to what I command

you and do not subtract from it, but keep the commands of the Lord your God that I give you....

See, I have taught you decrees and laws as the Lord my God commanded me, so that you may follow them in the land you are entering to take possession of it. Observe them carefully, for this will show your wisdom and understanding to the nations, who will hear about all these decrees and say, "Surely this great nation is a wise and understanding people." What other nation is so great as to have their gods near them the way the Lord our God is near us whenever we pray to him? And what other nation is so great as to have such righteous decrees and laws as this body of laws I am setting before you today?

Only be careful, and watch yourselves closely so that you do not forget the things your eyes have seen or let them fade from your heart as long as you live. Teach them to your children and to their children after them. (Deut. 4:1-2,5-9 NIV)

Leaders should not be hesitant or timid about speaking God's truth. Leaders should not ask, "What will my people think of me? What will the media say about me? If I speak God's truth, won't I be mocked and criticized?"

Authentic leaders should *expect* to be mocked and criticized. Godly leaders, bold leaders, should speak God's truth regardless of attacks and criticism. If you don't want to be mocked, if you don't want to be criticized, stay away from leadership. It's that simple.

Moses was mocked by his enemies and criticized by his own people. He continued to speak God's truth. So should we.

EIGHTH LESSON: *Bold leaders are always mentoring young leaders.*

Moses chose Joshua as his successor and mentored him because he had the makings of a strong, bold leader. Joshua had shown great skill, courage, and boldness as a military strategist. He had shown great faith in God when he and Caleb spied out the promised land.

In Exodus 17, Joshua led the attack against Amalekites. After the Israelites won the victory, the Lord told Moses, "Write this on a scroll as something to be remembered and make sure that Joshua hears it." Why? Because God wanted to encourage Joshua by commemorating his brave leadership. The scroll of Joshua's deeds would become part of the enduring history of the Israelite people.

In Exodus 24, we see another mentoring moment between Moses and Joshua. Moses takes Joshua under his wing and brings him along at a key moment in his leadership journey. God tells Moses to come up on the mountain, and He will give Moses tablets of stone with the Law and the Commandments. So Moses sets out with Joshua at his side, and together they hike up the mountain. There, the glory of God surrounds them like a fiery cloud. Moses stays on the mountain for forty days and forty nights with Joshua camped nearby. During those days on the mountaintop with Moses, Joshua learns how to listen for God's leading, how to hear his voice, and how to meet him in prayer.

While Moses and Joshua were up on the mountain, the Israelites fell into disobedience and idolatry down below. Even Moses's brother Aaron got swept up in the idolatrous fervor and helped the people melt their jewelry into a golden calf. When Moses and Joshua start down the mountain with the tablets of God's commandments, they hear noises and shouting from the camp below. Joshua, a warrior who is always alert to the sounds of war, jumps to a mistaken conclusion. "There is the sound of war in the camp," he said.

But Moses corrected Joshua, reminding him that it's a mistake for a leader to judge a situation too hastily. "It is not the sound of victory," Moses said, "it is not the sound of defeat; it is the sound of singing that I hear" (Exod. 32:15-18 NIV).

Mentors must sometimes correct their protégés and help them learn how to control their hasty impulses and rash judgments. Wise mentors know that young leaders must be given opportunities to serve. We should never push young leaders into too much responsibility too early, but we should give them leadership experiences, a little at a time, to help them grow.

There is a scene in Numbers 11 where Moses prays that a measure of God's Spirit that rests upon him would also be given to the seventy elders of the Israelites. These elders then begin to prophesy in the camp, just as Moses himself had prophesied. When Joshua saw that these elders were prophesying, he felt that they were infringing on the leadership role of Moses. Joshua thought only Moses should prophesy, so he impetuously ran to Moses and said, "Moses, my lord, stop them!"

But Moses rebuked Joshua and said, "Are you jealous for my sake? I wish that all the Lord's people were prophets and that the Lord would put his Spirit on them!"

Joshua learned a lesson in humility that day.

These are just a few of the ways of Moses trained and mentored Joshua as his successor. As someone once observed, the goal of leadership is not to create more followers but to create more leaders. Moses trained Joshua for leadership, and he trained him well.

When it was time for Moses to climb the last mountain, take one last look at the promised land, and breathe his last breath, Moses knew he had done all he could to bring his people home. The rest of the journey belonged to Joshua and his generation. Moses died at peace. He had left the nation of Israel in capable hands.

THE BUCK STOPS HERE

Harry S. Truman was born in Lamar, Missouri, on May 8, 1884. As a boy, he was very close to his mother, who encouraged his interests in reading and music. When Truman was six, his family moved to Independence, Missouri. After graduating from high school in 1901, he hoped to attend the Military Academy at West Point, but was barred due to poor eyesight. In 1905, Truman joined the Missouri Army National Guard (he passed the vision exam by memorizing the eye chart).

When the U.S. entered World War I, Truman was commissioned a captain and put in charge of an artillery battery that was infamous for disciplinary problems—D Battery, 129th Field Artillery, 60th Brigade, 35th Infantry Division. Truman said, "I called all the sergeants and corporals together. I told them I knew they had been making trouble for the previous commanders. I said, 'I didn't come over here to get along with you. You've got to get along with me.' ... We got along."

The evening of August 29, 1918, D Battery took a position on a mountainside in eastern France, near the German-French border. Two of Truman's men pulled the horses back a couple of hundred yards, and D Battery unleashed a barrage of high explosive rounds. The men with the horses were supposed to return when the last round was fired, so the horses could pull the artillery piece out of range of German artillery. Half an hour after the barrage ended, the soldiers hadn't returned with the horses.

Furious, Truman ordered his artillerymen to lug the artillery piece out by hand. Then he climbed on his horse, intending to find the missing men—but his horse stumbled in a hole and fell, rolling over onto Truman. At that moment, German artillery shells screamed down from the sky and exploded close by. Truman knew those shells contained poison gas.

While clawing his way out from under the horse, he heard his panicked sergeant shout, "Run, boys! They've got a bracket on us!" The sergeant's panic spread quickly, and the men fled.

Truman yelled at his men, calling them every name in the book, ordering them back to their posts. The soldiers came back, shamefaced, and pulled the guns out of harm's way. Truman later commended his men (except the sergeant) for cool courage under fire (in truth, they feared Truman more than the German poison gas).

Where did Harry Truman learn the art of clear-headed, bold decision making under fire? How did he acquire the Sixth Side of Leadership? He acquired that quality because he had to. It was his job to protect the artillery piece and by hook or by crook, he was going to do his job.

Captain Harry S. Truman got the men of D Battery safely through the war. Not a single man was wounded or killed. For the rest of their lives, the veterans of D Battery were loyal to Harry Truman, the bold leader who demonstrated bold physical courage under fire. Truman learned that both courage and cowardice are contagious—and he was determined that his own courage would be more infectious than his sergeant's panic.

Truman emerged from World War I a proven leader, ready to shoulder the backbreaking, soul-destroying burdens of the presidency during World War II. On April 12, 1945, after serving as Vice President for less than a hundred days, Truman was informed that

President Roosevelt had died of a massive stroke. Truman was now "Mr. President."

The day after taking office, Truman told reporters, "Boys, if you ever pray, pray for me now. I don't know if you fellas ever had a load of hay fall on you, but when they told me what happened yesterday, I felt like the moon, the stars, and all the planets had fallen on me."

A few days after being sworn in, Truman was told for the first time of a newly developed secret weapon, the atomic bomb. He made the decision to use atomic bombs against Hiroshima and Nagasaki. As a result, Japan surrendered, and a bloody invasion that might have cost millions of lives was averted.

After the war, Truman faced many tough decisions as he dealt with record high inflation, a crippling railway strike, the Marshall Plan, the Berlin Airlift, the founding of the United Nations, the Korean War, and much more. Though Truman appeared to make decisions boldly and without hesitation, historian Alan Axelrod observed that Truman never acted in haste:

> He was so incisive and absolute a decision maker that it often appeared as if he breezed through the process. He was not a man who agonized, at least not visibly. The president's job, Truman believed, was to make decisions, and he was very good at his job. Instead of a nameplate on his desk, he had his famous sign proclaiming, "The Buck Stops Here." He explained in 1952 ... "The president—whoever he is— has to decide. He can't pass the buck to anybody...."

That's bold leadership. A bold leader dares to take prudent, calculated risks in order to achieve important goals. A bold leader dares to make a decision, knowing that even a bad decision is better than failing to decide. A bold leader dares to accept responsibility for his decisions, secure in the knowledge that it was the best decision possible at the time.

Above all, a bold leader seeks the will and the wisdom of God before making any decision. Leadership is not about doing what's popular or doing what's easy. It's about doing what's right. To be a great leader, be a *complete* leader. Build the Sixth Side of Leadership into your life. *Be bold.*

CHAPTER 7: QUESTIONS FOR REFLECTION AND DISCUSSION

1. When God called Moses to lead the Israelites, Moses felt a deep sense of reluctance and inadequacy. Can you identify with Moses's self-doubt?

   How did Moses overcome his insecurities? What lessons do you see for your own leadership life in the example of young Moses and his transition from a timid youth to a bold leader?

2. Moses became a bold leader who dared to challenge Pharaoh, who dared to lead his people south when the logical path led north, who dared to trust God for a miracle at the Red Sea, and who dared to ascend a mountain to meet God face-to-face. It's hard to believe this is the same young man who quaked in his sandals before the burning bush.

   Can you recall a time in your leadership experience when the situation demanded more boldness, faith, and courage than you could muster? What did you do? How did it turn out? What lessons did you learn? What would you do differently if you could do it over again?

3. Bold leaders overcome self-doubt by trusting in God, not in themselves. When Moses stood before the burning bush, he asked God, "Who am I that I should go to Pharaoh and bring the Israelites out of Egypt?"

   Have you ever faced a challenge that was bigger than you could handle? Did that challenge defeat you? Or did the sufficiency of God enable you to rise to the challenge? What did you learn from that experience?

4. Bold leaders trust God—and keep moving. They don't sit and wait passively for God to act; they translate faith into action. How would you apply this insight to your own leadership challenges today? Have you ever waited for a miracle from God only to discover that God wanted you to get up and get going?

5. Boldness is contagious—and so is fear. That's why it's important for leaders to demonstrate bold courage to their followers. If the leader appears unsure—or worse, panicked—fear will spread throughout the organization. Have you ever experienced (either as a leader or a subordinate) a situation where the leader's lack of boldness led to failure? Or where the leader's contagious confidence saved the day? What lessons can you learn from the bold confidence of Moses?

6. Bold leaders should never go it alone. They need wise counselors to help keep their boldness from turning into recklessness, to keep their egos in check, and to remind them to maintain moral firewalls. Moses had wise counselors, and he listened humbly to their advice. Who are your counselors? Are you accountable to them? Are you transparent and honest with them?

7. Moses selected a bold young leader-in-training—Joshua—to be his successor. Moses mentored this energetic young man and taught him to trust God and dare great things for Him. Do you have a "Joshua," someone you are mentoring and training as a future bold leader? What lessons do you learn from Moses that enable you to be a better mentor to your "Joshua"?

CHAPTER 8

QUEEN ESTHER: LEADING BY SERVING

Truett Cathy started his first business in 1929. He was eight years old, and his front yard Coca-Cola stand gave him his first taste of entrepreneurial success.

Three years later, Truett got a job delivering newspapers for the *Atlanta Journal*. He started with the philosophy that success is built on excellent customer service. He made sure that every newspaper was exactly where the customer wanted it—never in the bushes or the gutter. For seven years, he was one of the *Journal's* top paper carriers.

On May 23, 1946, Truett and his brother Ben opened The Dwarf Grill (later renamed The Dwarf House) in the Atlanta suburb of Hapeville. The quaint architecture featured (in addition to a full-sized entrance) a small round-top red door, just the right size for children or dwarfs. Truett trained his servers to deliver excellent, friendly service. His goal was to always exceed customer expectations.

Five years later, Truett opened a second Dwarf House in Forest Park, and there he perfected the recipe for a white meat chicken sandwich he called "The Chick-fil-A." He based the recipe on cooking techniques learned from his mother, a former boarding house cook. Truett would later trademark the name of this popular sandwich.

In 1967, Truett Cathy opened a new restaurant in Greenbriar Mall. This time "Chick-fil-A" was not just a menu item—it was the name of the restaurant. This would be the first of hundreds of Chick-fil-A restaurants.

Throughout his career, Truett maintained a closed-on-Sunday policy. A devout Christian, Truett believed the Lord's Day is a day of rest—and giving his employees a day of rest was his way of serving his employees as well as serving the Lord. When a shopping mall developer offered Truett a sizable donation to the church of his choice if he would remain open on Sundays, Truett politely said no.

In the 1970s, he introduced the Team Member Scholarship program to help employees continue their education. The program has benefited thousands of young Chick-fil-A workers over the years.

The Chick-fil-A restaurant chain grew and grew, spreading nationwide. In 2001, Chick-fil-A opened its one-thousandth location. In 2012, Chick-fil-A surpassed KFC as the nation's number one chicken restaurant chain. Truett Cathy's company achieved amazing success because he was a leader who believed in serving—serving his customers, serving his employees, and serving his franchisees.

Though Truett was a devout Christian, and he learned servant leadership by studying the life of Christ, he didn't demand that his employees be Christians. He only expected them to exemplify the traits of the Chick-fil-A culture—traits of humility, compassion, sincerity, and a serving heart. Managers were expected to treat both customers and employees according to these principles. As a result, Chick-fil-A restaurants became known as a great place to work, especially for young people needing entry-level employment.

Truett Cathy passed away on September 8, 2014. Throughout his leadership career, he exemplified what it means to lead by serving. He was an excellent role model in the business world of the Seventh

Side of Leadership: A Serving Heart. As John Stott, the Anglican preacher, once said, "Leaders have power, but power is safe only in the hands of those who humble themselves to serve."

FOR SUCH A TIME AS THIS

When I think of servant leadership, I think of Queen Esther.

Esther was a young Jewish orphan-in-exile who rose to become the most powerful woman in the ancient world—Queen Esther of Persia. She demonstrated many great leadership qualities, and perhaps exhibited most, if not all, Seven Sides of Leadership. She was a persuasive communicator, a bold and strategic risk-taker, and a woman of competence, character, and great people skills.

But above all, Queen Esther had the heart of a servant.

The events in the Book of Esther take place during Israel's exile, after the Babylonian Empire has been conquered by Persia. There are parallels between the Book of Esther and other historical accounts, including *The Histories of Herodotus* and the Old Testament Book of Nehemiah.

In Nehemiah 2, for example, there is a scene where Nehemiah goes before the King of Persia to ask permission to go to his homeland and rebuild Jerusalem. In verse 6, Nehemiah says, "Then the king, with the queen sitting beside him, asked me, 'How long will your journey take, and when will you get back?'" Many Bible scholars believe that this significant detail—"with the queen sitting beside him"—refers to Queen Esther, and suggests that the King might have been influenced in Nehemiah's favor by the Jewish queen of the Persian realm.

The Book of Esther is set in Persia (modern-day Iran). It's the story of the origin of the Jewish festival of Purim—a celebration of deliverance from a genocidal plot against the Jews nearly 2,500 years ago.

Even though God is never directly mentioned in this book, the unseen hand of God is everywhere in this book, controlling events, moving people into positions of influence, and instilling courage in a young queen's heart. Some Bible scholars believe God's name was deliberately left out of the book because it was an official document of the Persian Empire. Copies were distributed throughout the realm. Had it contained the name of the God of the Jews, translations into other languages might have substituted the name of some false god in place of the one true God. The writer of the Book of Esther wanted to ensure that idolatry would never find its way into the book.

The story opens in the royal palace of Susa, capital of the Persian Empire. King Xerxes is hosting a six-month celebration of the power and wealth of his kingdom. One night, after the King has been drinking too much, he orders his servants to bring Queen Vashti to the banquet hall. He wants to put her beauty on display for his guests, but proud Queen Vashti refuses. An angry King Xerxes banishes and divorces her, then issues a proclamation ordering all the most beautiful virgins of the kingdom be brought before him. He will select one of these young women as his new queen.

Among the young women who answer the King's summons is a beautiful Jewish woman named Hadassah. She was born in the community of exiled Jews in Persia, and has never seen her ancestral homeland. She has been raised to act and speak like a Persian, yet she has been taught the history and culture of the Jews. Though her birth name was Hadassah, she took the Persian name Esther to shield herself from anti-Jewish prejudice. Her parents are dead and she has been raised by her cousin Mordecai.

Esther, acting under instructions from Mordecai, goes before the King and wins his favor. King Xerxes chooses her as his queen. On Mordecai's advice, she hides the fact that she is Jewish, and the King assumes she is Persian. The King's ignorance of her Jewish heritage eventually becomes a key factor in the story.

Later, Mordecai discovers a plot to assassinate the King, so he sends word to the King through Queen Esther. As a result, the conspirators are caught and executed, and Mordecai's role in protecting the King is recorded in the Annals of the Kingdom.

In Esther 3, we meet the villain of the story—Haman the Agagite, the prime minister—a powerful figure in the Persian government, with an ego to match. On one occasion, Haman demands that Mordecai bow and kneel in homage to him, but Mordecai refuses. Later, when Haman discovers that Mordecai is Jewish, he takes an oath to destroy Mordecai and all of his people, the Jews. Consumed with hatred, he takes his case to the King:

> Haman said to King Xerxes, "There is a certain people dispersed and scattered among the peoples in all the provinces of your kingdom whose customs are different from those of all other people and who do not obey the king's laws; it is not in the king's best interest to tolerate them." (Esther 3:8 NIV)

Haman persuades King Xerxes to destroy the Jewish people. So the king issues an order to annihilate all the Jews—including women and children—and to plunder their possessions. This holocaust is to take place on a single day—the thirteenth day of Adar, the twelfth month. While issuing the order, King Xerxes is unaware that his own wife, Queen Esther, is a Jew.

Anguished over the pending holocaust, Mordecai puts on sackcloth and ashes as a sign of mourning. Then he sends word to

Esther of Haman's plot, urging her to go to the King and plead for mercy for the Jews.

In reply, Esther tells Mordecai that, according to Persian law, any person who approaches the King without being summoned will face execution. The only exception is if the King raises the golden scepter and spares that person's life. Even the Queen is subject to the law. Mordecai reads Esther's message, then replies:

> Do not think that because you are in the king's house you alone of all the Jews will escape. For if you remain silent at this time, relief and deliverance for the Jews will arise from another place, but you and your father's family will perish. And who knows but that you have come to royal position for such a time as this? (Esther 4:13b-14 NIV)

Mordecai's logic is unassailable. Yes, Queen Esther risks her life if she goes before the King without being summoned. But she is already under a death sentence because of the King's decree. If she plays it safe and remains silent, there's a good chance she'll be executed with the rest of her people. But, Mordecai adds, even if Esther remains silent, rescue for the Jews will "arise from another place." Though Mordecai does not say "God," that is clearly what he means.

In other words, God will deliver the Jews from death one way or another. Queen Esther can choose to be a part of God's plan to rescue her people—or she can remain silent and miss the opportunity to be used by God. Then Mordecai adds one last argument: "And who knows but that you have come to royal position for such a time as this?"

Esther had to decide whether to say yes to God's will—or do nothing. To paraphrase Edmund Burke, all that is necessary for evil to triumph is for good people to do nothing. Esther chose to say yes.

In that moment, she chose to lead by serving. Esther sent another message to Mordecai:

> Go, gather together all the Jews who are in Susa, and fast for me. Do not eat or drink for three days, night or day. I and my maids will fast as you do. When this is done, I will go to the king, even though it is against the law. And if I perish, I perish. (Esther 4:16 NIV)

After three days of fasting and prayer, Esther dressed in her royal robes and strode to the King's hall. In spite of going without food or drink for three days, Queen Esther is radiant, and the King is captivated by her. He says, "What is your request? Even up to half the kingdom, it will be given you."

This might seem like the ideal moment to make her request known. The King has just invited her to ask him for anything. Yet Queen Esther waits. She instinctively knows it's not the right time. Instead of asking the King for a favor, she invites him to a banquet— and she invites Haman, too. During her fast, God had given her a plan that would expose the evil schemes of Haman.

The King and Queen go to the banquet. Once again, King Xerxes is captivated by the Queen's grace and beauty, and he again asks if there is anything she wants. She says, "Let the king and Haman come tomorrow to the banquet I will prepare for them. Then I will answer the king's question."

This turn of events fills Haman with pride and arrogance. He believes he has won the confidence of the King and Queen. Leaving the banquet, he goes to Mordecai and demands that Mordecai bow to him—and Mordecai again refuses.

Infuriated, Haman complains about Mordecai to his wife and friends, and they tell him that he should simply get rid of Mordecai.

Construct a tall wooden gibbet (an impaling stake) and execute Mordecai on it. Haman thought it was an excellent idea.

That same night, King Xerxes is unable to sleep. To cure his insomnia, the king asks his servants to bring him the Annals of the Kingdom. As the servant reads from the book, the king hears how Mordecai warned him of the plot against his life. The king realizes that Mordecai has never been recognized for saving the king's life.

Just then—in God's perfect timing—Haman approaches the hall of the king. He plans to ask the king to order the hanging of Mordecai. As Haman comes into the royal presence, King Xerxes ask, "What should be done for the man the King delights to honor?"

What happens next is simply hilarious: Haman thinks the king wants to honor *him*. He has no idea that the king wants to honor Mordecai. So Haman is popping his buttons with pride as he answers:

> For the man the king delights to honor, have them bring a royal robe the king has worn and a horse the king has ridden, one with a royal crest placed on its head. Then let the robe and horse be entrusted to one of the king's most noble princes. Let them robe the man the king delights to honor, and lead him on the horse through the city streets, proclaiming before him, 'This is what is done for the man the king delights to honor!' (Esther 6:7b-9 NIV)

Haman has just described the kind of honor he wants for himself. The King, however, thinks Haman's suggestion is a fitting reward for Mordecai. As a result, the Scriptures tell us:

> "Go at once," the King commanded Haman. "Get the robe and the horse and do just as you have suggested for Mordecai the Jew, who sits at the king's gate. Do not neglect anything you have recommended." (Esther 6:10 NIV)

Picture the shock and dismay on Haman's face! The King had just ordered him to honor the very man Haman wanted to execute. But what choice did he have? He grudgingly carried out the King's command.

That night, King Xerxes, Esther, and Haman gather again for dinner. During dinner, the King again asks, "Queen Esther, what is your request? Even up to half the kingdom, it will be granted."

"If it pleases you, Your Majesty, grant me my life and spare my people. For I and my people have been sold to be destroyed, killed and annihilated."

Shocked and furious, King Xerxes asks, "Who is he? Where is the man who has dared to do such a thing?"

Queen Esther points. "He's right here—an adversary and enemy, this vile Haman."

The King stands in rage and strides into the garden as Haman quails in terror. Haman knows the king has decided his fate, so he rushes to Queen Esther's side to beg for his life. When the king returns, he sees Haman with his hands on the Queen.

Infuriated, the king calls the guards, who take Haman into custody. The king orders the guards to impale Haman on the gibbet he has constructed for Mordecai. So the guards carry out the king's command.

King Xerxes exalts Mordecai to the same position previously held by Haman. Under Persian law, the King cannot rescind his earlier edict of death against the Jews. But he can do the next best thing. He authorizes Mordecai to issue a new proclamation permitting the Jews to use deadly force to protect themselves.

When the appointed day of the holocaust comes, five hundred attackers and Haman's ten sons die in Susa, and seventy-five thousand attackers are killed by the Jews across Persia. The Jews take no plunder—they act purely in self-defense. Esther then sends a letter establishing an annual commemoration of the redemption of the Jewish people, a festival called Purim.

The Jewish people triumphed because Queen Esther made the courageous decision to lead by serving—to lay down her life, if necessary, to defend her people.

LESSONS IN SERVANT LEADERSHIP FROM QUEEN ESTHER

The story of Queen Esther is rich in lessons in how to lead by serving and serve by leading. At the beginning of the story, Queen Esther was young and inexperienced in her leadership role. She was frightened and reluctant, and her cousin Mordecai had to coach her in her role and her moral responsibility. But once she accepted her role, she discovered depths of wisdom, character, and courage she never knew she had—and in the process, she became a leader. Here are some lessons we can learn from Queen Esther's leadership journey:

FIRST LESSON: *Servant leaders risk their own lives for the sake of their followers.*

Servanthood is the essence of unselfishness. A leader must put serving ahead of safety. This is a lesson Queen Esther didn't understand at first. But Mordecai told her that if she tried to save her life, she would lose it. God would find a way to rescue His people—but Queen Esther, by her silence, would pass up the opportunity to be used by God as His instrument of redemption.

Mordecai helped Queen Esther realize that God had chosen her and elevated her to a leadership position "for such a time as this." Once Queen Esther accepted her role as a servant leader, she put her life 100 percent on the line. She was ready to die to serve her people.

SECOND LESSON: *Servant leaders put God's law above human law.*

In Acts 5:29, Peter and the other apostles tell the Sanhedrin, "We must obey God rather than human beings." Queen Esther decided to disobey Persian law and go before her husband, the King, without an official summons. "If I die, I die," she said. This sounds like a fatalistic or pessimistic statement—but in context we see that it is really a statement of conviction and determination. She was going to carry out her mission, regardless of the cost, even the cost of her own life.

Queen Esther was on a mission to save her people from genocide. The lives of the Jewish people were worth infinitely more than an official protocol. It came down to a choice between obeying human law and obeying God's law. There was only one decision to make— and she made it.

THIRD LESSON: *When your moment of opportunity arrives, you won't feel ready—but serve anyway.*

Queen Esther felt completely unprepared for the challenge she faced. She didn't know what to say or how to approach the King—and she knew that any little mistake could result in her death. She was young, she was scared, and she was insecure. Yet here was an opportunity— and the lives of her people depended on her. She probably thought, "I can't do this! I'll make a mess of things! I'll get myself killed—and my people with me."

Yet God had been preparing her for such a time as this. Opportunity was knocking, and this was no time to hide behind the door.

Does this situation sound familiar? Have you ever faced a situation where you sensed God calling you to step up and lead, to step forward and serve—but you hesitated, paralyzed by fear and insecurity? No one feels ready when the moment of crisis comes. There is always that sinking feeling, that moment of self-doubt when you ask yourself, "Am I up to this challenge? What if I make the wrong decision? People are counting on me. What if I let them down?"

If you don't rise to this leadership challenge, who will? If you are not ready, who else is? Remember the example of Queen Esther. She didn't feel ready—but she stepped up and led anyway. That's what servant leaders do.

FOURTH LESSON: *Serving leaders often spend a lot of time in obscurity and preparation.*

There's very little glory or fame in being a servant. Leaders who serve are often invisible and anonymous for much of their lives. Esther experienced this kind of invisibility even as Queen of Persia.

Though she was the Queen, she had no power of her own. The only way she could influence events was by influencing the heart of the king. And the king would often go days or weeks without requiring Queen Esther's presence. During those times away from the king, she was invisible and powerless. She had no influence. That was why Mordecai urged her to take the life-or-death risk of going before the king uninvited.

During those times of invisibility, she devoted herself to preparing herself for the challenge ahead. She prayed and fasted, and she asked others to pray and fast. She knew that she would need to be well-prepared in body, mind, and spirit before going to face the king.

When you find yourself in a state of preparation and obscurity, use that time wisely. Prepare yourself for the leadership opportunities and challenges that await you. Pray for opportunities to learn and grow. Seek out a "Mordecai" of your own—a wise teacher and spiritual mentor who will encourage you, challenge you, and push you to achieve more than you think is possible.

God has gifted you and equipped you to be a servant and a leader for such a time as this. Ask God to throw you into the deep end of life, so that you can learn to "swim" as a servant leader. At the same time, be patient during your waiting time, your growing time, your training time, your period of obscurity and invisibility. God will use you in a powerful way if you are patient and open to the opportunities He will show you.

FIFTH LESSON: *The two most important ingredients of servant leadership are humility and love.*

A serving heart is a humble heart. Edwin Louis Cole, author of *Strong Men in Tough Times*, put it this way: "You can only lead to the degree you are willing to serve.... The more you serve, the greater you become. Many people today consider the status of a servant to be demeaning, but in God's kingdom, instead of being appointed to lead, we are anointed to serve."[32]

When Jesus trained the Twelve to be leaders, he taught them by word and example that they should be servants, not bosses: "Whoever wants to become great among you must be your servant" (Matt. 20:26 NIV). Are we truly servants? Are we willing to sacrifice ourselves—our comfort, our finances, our position, our reputations, and even our lives—for the sake of the people we lead? Are we willing to humble ourselves and follow the leadership model of Jesus, the leadership model of Queen Esther?

Jesus took a basin and towel, and He humbled himself to wash the dirty feet of eleven true disciples and one traitor. By becoming a servant, He transformed the world.

Great coaches lead their players by loving them. Eddie Robinson, the longtime football coach at Grambling State University, said in his autobiography, "You can't coach a person unless you love him. I loved these guys and looked at them as though they were the ones I wanted to marry my daughter."[33]

During a speech in Charlotte, North Carolina, I quoted those words by Coach Robinson. After my talk, a woman introduced herself and said, "In the late 1990s, I was in a waiting room at the Green Clinic in Ruston, Louisiana, near the Grambling campus. I noticed Coach Eddie Robinson in the waiting room, so I asked him, 'Coach, what advice would you have for someone like me?' He said, 'Love everybody, and do it out loud.' I thought that was the best advice I had ever heard. Now, I'm not a tattoo gal, but I do carry this reminder of what Coach Robinson said to me that day."

She pulled her sleeve back and showed me a tattoo on her right wrist. It was very small, and I had to put on my glasses to examine it. There were no words, just a very small tattooed heart. "It's just a reminder of Coach Robinson's words to me—'Love everybody, and do it out loud.' I've been trying to follow his advice ever since."

That's great leadership advice, because it's all about being a servant to others.

Jim Cymbala is pastor of The Brooklyn Tabernacle, a megachurch that meets in a renovated theater in downtown Brooklyn, New York. Jim has written several books, including *Fresh Wind, Fresh Fire*, and his wife Carol directs the Grammy-winning Brooklyn Tabernacle Choir. He was recently a guest preacher at our church, First Baptist of Orlando.

His message was simple: As Christians, are we known by our love? When people come into your church or my church, do they feel loved? Many people go through their daily lives feeling unloved, uncared-for. That Sunday morning church service may be the only time in their week when they might experience the love of God and the Christian love of other people. So what is the temperature of love in your church? That was Jim Cymbala's message.

At the end of the service, he said, "Now, I'm going to give you a Brooklyn Tab closing. Men, look around you and find five men in the congregation, then hug them and tell them, 'I love you in the Lord!' And ladies, look around you and find five other women, then hug them and say, 'I love you in the Lord!' That's how we close our services at The Brooklyn Tab."

I have to say, I felt a little strange. I looked around, and all the men around me seemed a little uncomfortable. But within seconds, all across the sanctuary, men were embracing other men, and saying, "I love you in the Lord." And women were embracing each other, and saying, "I love you in the Lord." And every time I hugged another man in the congregation and said those words, it got a little easier. That's how our service ended, and our congregation will never forget that.

Now, Christian love is not just hugging people and saying, "I love you in the Lord." It's not just a warm feeling. That's not what Jim was telling us. Christian love is putting yourself on the line for other people, sacrificing your time and comfort for other people, showing grace to other people and forgiving them when they hurt us. Love is a choice, not a warm-fuzzy feeling.

But there's nothing wrong with that warm feeling. Why shouldn't real Christian love begin with a hug and some loving words? Take that first step of loving other people in your church, even if it feels awkward. Make sure you love people, and do it out loud.

THE COMPLETE LEADER

God does not need you or me in order to accomplish His will on earth. He doesn't need anybody. But we need Him—and I'm eternally grateful that He has chosen to use human beings like you and me to serve His purpose. Doing His will, obeying His commandments, and serving His cause gives meaning to our lives and to our leadership.

Mordecai told Queen Esther she could refuse God's call, and He would accomplish His purpose one way or another—but she would miss out on the joy of serving. If she tried to save her life, she would lose it. But if she would put her life on the line to answer God's call, she would save it. And that's the lesson of Queen Esther's life for you and me.

As Christians, as leaders, we know that God has called us to take part in His business in history—but the business of God is a risky business. Sometimes, to be a leader and a servant in obedience to God means putting everything on the line, including life itself. A leader with a serving heart is not afraid to die in the line of duty.

Are you familiar with the history of the island of Molokai in the Hawaiian Islands chain? Today, Molokai is a paradise. But in the mid-nineteenth century, an epidemic of leprosy swept the Hawaiian Islands, and victims of the disease (which was incurable in those days) were quarantined on the island of Molokai.

Ships with leprosy sufferers would anchor off-shore, and the sick were forced overboard. Some drowned, but others swam to shore. Condemned and without hope, they lived in caves or in grass huts. Supply ships occasionally tossed crates of food into the water for the currents to wash ashore.

A Belgian priest, Father Damien de Veuster, learned of the plight of the Molokai lepers, and he volunteered to serve them. In 1873, Father Damien waded ashore and walked up onto the beach. He was thirty-three years old and he was skilled in carpentry and medicine. He lived among the lepers, teaching them how to build houses with wood. He preached to them about the love of Jesus and prayed with them. He treated their wounds and helped them bury their dead.

For a dozen years, he lived among the leprosy sufferers, and seemed immune to the disease. Then, one night, he filled a basin with steaming hot water. He had a pitcher of cold water nearby, and intended to mix the cold with the hot to a comfortable temperature. He put his feet into the steaming water—then yanked them out, remembering he had forgotten to add cold water.

Then he realized he felt no pain. Leprosy is a nerve-destroying disease that deprives its sufferers of sensation, including the sense of pain. Father Damien knew why he felt no pain.

The next time Father Damien stood before his congregation to preach, he began his sermon with the words, "We lepers—"

Like Queen Esther, like Jesus, Father Damien led by serving. He went to hopeless people and gave them hope. He lived among them and took their disease into himself. A true servant, with a heart full of love, he was willing to die for the people he led.

Death came for him in 1889, when he was forty-nine years old. He lived the life—and died the death—of a servant leader. He was a complete leader, a leader with the serving heart.

The Seventh Side of Leadership is the one quality, more than any other, that will make you complete as a leader. Be a servant who leads. Be a leader who serves. Be a leader with a serving heart.

CHAPTER 8: QUESTIONS FOR REFLECTION AND DISCUSSION

1. Queen Esther was a leader with a serving heart. She put serving ahead of safety. Queen Esther didn't understand this principle at first, but Mordecai helped her see that God had chosen her and elevated her to a leadership role "for such a time as this." Once she accepted that role, she bravely and selflessly put her life on the line.

   Do you identify with Esther? In your leadership arena, do you believe God has placed you in that role to play a critical part "for such a time as this"? Do you sense God calling you to make selfless sacrifices to serve the people you lead?

2. Servant leaders put God's law above human law. A leader with a serving heart says, "I must obey God rather than human beings." At the risk of her life, Queen Esther disobeyed Persian law to obey God and serve her people. Have you ever felt God calling you to violate rules and traditions, or even break the law, to serve God and serve your people? What was the result when you did that? What did it cost you? Was it worth it? Do you have any regrets?

3. Queen Esther felt unprepared for the challenge. She was young, insecure, and frightened, yet she stepped up, risked everything, and served her people. From Queen Esther's example, we learn that when our opportunity arises, we won't feel ready—but we should serve anyway.

   Can you recall a time when you faced a crisis, a decision, or a challenge that you were completely unprepared to undertake? How did you respond? How *should* you have responded, in view of Queen Esther's example? What was the result of your choice? If you could do it over again, how would you respond to the challenge?

4. Serving leaders frequently spend a lot of time in obscurity and preparation. They are often anonymous and invisible for years. During her time of preparation, Queen Esther prayed and fasted, and asked others to pray and fast.

   What lessons and insights do you draw about your own leadership role and leadership challenges from the example of Queen Esther? What steps do you need to take this week to be morally, spiritually, and physically prepared for the challenges you face?

5. Queen Esther could not have saved her people without the wise insight, encouragement, and coaching of Mordecai. He helped her find her courage and confidence. He helped her sort through options and strategies. Who is your "Mordecai"? Who is the person who knows you through and through, the one person you can go to, confess any fault or sin, and receive encouragement and counsel?

6. The two key ingredients of servant leadership are humility and love. Are you willing to humble yourself and become a person of no reputation to serve the people you lead?

   Do the people you lead see you as a humble servant—or an arrogant boss? Do they know you love them? Why or why not?

   What are some specific actions you can take this week to demonstrate genuine humility and love in your leadership role?

STEP UP AND LEAD

Over the years, I've had the privilege of being in the presence of some of the greatest leaders of our time—presidents, civil rights leaders, foreign dignitaries, corporate CEOs, coaches, and media figures. Whenever I have encountered a genuine seven-sided leader, I have sensed it almost immediately.

When you encounter someone who is complete in all Seven Sides of Leadership, and especially when that person is committed to serving God and leading God's way, brace for impact. That encounter is going to change you and mark your life forever.

THE FIRST SIDE OF LEADERSHIP IS *Vision.*

When you encounter a godly leader of vision, you find yourself in the presence of someone who looks toward the horizon of God's will, who seeks the mind of God before making his or her own plans, and who cooperates with God in fulfilling His plan for eternity. Open your heart to God in prayer. Ask Him to place His vision before your eyes. Then commit yourself to obediently playing your part in turning that vision into reality.

THE SECOND SIDE OF LEADERSHIP IS *Communication.*

Take the vision God has placed before you, and shout it to the world. Communicate it in your family, in your neighborhood, at your office, on your campus, in your church, across the Internet, and around the world. Communicate the vision, and spread the good news of Jesus Christ wherever you go.

THE THIRD SIDE OF LEADERSHIP IS *People Skills.*

There are many skills that make up the category we call People Skills, including listening skills, collaborating skills, the ability to value differences, open-mindedness, patience, tolerance, empathy, poise in a crisis, courtesy, negotiating skills, conflict-resolution skills, and a sense of humor, But the greatest people skill of all is *love*—the skill of unconditionally seeking what is best for everyone around you, even those who are unlikeable and unlovable. Make sure that the love of Jesus Christ radiates from you to everyone you meet. If you do that, all the other people skills will naturally fall into place.

THE FOURTH SIDE OF LEADERSHIP IS *Character.*

Don't let anyone find a single crack in your integrity, your honesty, your dependability, your work ethic, or your courage. When people know they can depend on your character, they will trust you and follow you anywhere. When people trust you, they will buy into your vision, your goals, and your team or organization. Above all, when people trust your character, they will have confidence in your leadership.

THE FIFTH SIDE OF LEADERSHIP IS *Competence.*

Sharpen your skills as a problem solver, a team builder, a motivator, and an administrator. Pay your dues and learn the ropes. Read, study, grow. Seek out mentors and advisors who can help you improve your leadership skills. The more competent you are, the more confident your followers will be—and the more eager they will be to follow your lead.

THE SIXTH SIDE OF LEADERSHIP IS *Boldness.*

You don't have to have a loud voice to be a bold leader. You just need to be a leader who takes charge, takes risks, and takes responsibility for the outcome. If all a person ever does is "play it safe," how can he call himself a leader? An authentic leader must be bold. Pursue a bold vision, communicate a bold message, and make bold decisions—do all that, and you'll be a bold leader.

THE SEVENTH SIDE OF LEADERSHIP IS *A Serving Heart.*

Be humble, be selfless, and love others. Put yourself at risk for the sake of your people. Lay down your life for the sake of your friends. Lead by serving, and leave a legacy of servant leadership.

Be a complete leader—a leader who has it all. The Seven Sides of Leadership are essential to being a complete leader in every arena, from politics to business to academia to the military to the church. Whatever leadership arena God calls you to, make sure you have all Seven Sides of Leadership locked in place—and there will be no dream too extreme for you to achieve, in God's will, in His timing, and by His strength.

Great leaders change the world and shape the future—but the Seven Sides of Leadership shape the complete leader. We live in dangerous times. We often feel that there is a vacuum of leadership in the world and in the church. God does not want us to sit around and complain about the leadership gap in our world today. He wants us to step up and fill that gap. He wants us to lead, and he wants us to *lead His way.*

I first discovered my potential for leadership when I was at Wake Forest University in North Carolina. I was a catcher on the baseball team and active in the Monogram Club, the letterman's club on campus. Every year, the Monogram Club staged a freshman vs. varsity basketball game. Less than a week before the game, the president of the Monogram Club said to me, "Williams, you're in charge of the freshman-varsity game." I asked him what had been done so far to organize and promote the game.

"Nothing," he said. "You'd better get busy."

I had never organized a basketball game before. I didn't know where to begin. I quickly found out I had to get tickets printed, arrange for a halftime show, book a singer for the national anthem, arrange for a pep band, and launch a promotional blitz. That week, I learned how to delegate tasks to other people—a key leadership skill. Long story short, the game preparations and promotion came together very quickly—and the event was a stunning success. We had a packed house, the pregame and halftime events came off perfectly, and we got rave reviews.

I'll never forget the sense of exhilaration I felt at the end of that night. I woke up the next morning thinking, *I might like to do this for a career!* And, as it turned out, that's exactly what happened.

I have spent more than fifty years in professional sports, building teams, putting on shows, and promoting like mad. And it all began when the president of the Monogram Club poked me in the chest and said, "Williams, you're in charge."

I stepped up and led—because the president of the club gave me no choice. In the years that followed, I made a point of seeking out leadership opportunities, learning the principles of leadership from mentors and experts, reading books about leadership, studying the lives of great leaders, and preparing myself in every way possible for a lifetime of leadership. One thing I've learned through the years is that there are three crucial steps that every leader must take.

First, a leader must view himself or herself as a leader. The leader must be able to say, confidently and without equivocation, "I am a leader." Or, at the very least, "I want to be a leader."

Second, a leader must devote himself or herself to preparation and training as a leader. The leader must study the principles of leadership. A leader must seek out mentors. A leader must seek out growth opportunities.

Third, a leader must step up and lead. Leadership opportunities come to us all the time, yet we pass them up or turn them down. We say, "I'm not ready for the challenge. Wait until I'm more experienced, more confident." I say, don't wait, don't say no. Instead, take on the challenge that scares you. Attempt a challenge that is big enough to defeat you—*then make sure it doesn't.*

Step up and lead.

As you lead, keep building the Seven Sides of Leadership into your life. Keep studying the lives of great biblical leaders. Work on your areas of weakness. If you are not a very good public speaker, seek out training and accept challenges that will force you to become a better communicator. If you have character defects that could undermine your leadership role, ask a few close friends to hold you accountable for improving your good character. If you have a tendency to timidity or dithering over decisions, practice becoming more bold, decisive, and firm in your decision making.

There is no better way to build the Seven Sides of Leadership into your life than by seizing leadership opportunities, accepting leadership challenges, and practicing leading God's way.

So live the leadership adventure, my friend. Follow the example of great leaders of the Bible, especially the example of Jesus Himself. Be complete, be strong, be bold, be humble, be a servant.

Step up and lead God's way.

CONTACT

You can contact Pat Williams at:

Pat Williams
c/o Orlando Magic
8701 Maitland Summit Boulevard
Orlando, FL 32810

407.916.2404
pwilliams@orlandomagic.com

Visit Pat Williams's Web site at:
www.PatWilliams.com

If you would like to set up a speaking engagement for Pat Williams, please call or write his assistant, Andrew Herdliska, at the above address, or call him at 407-916-2401. Requests can also be faxed to 407-916-2986 or e-mailed to aherdliska@orlandomagic.com.

We would love to hear from you. Please send your comments about this book to Pat Williams at the above address. Thank you.

ENDNOTES

1   Associated Press, "Hospital Is Visited by Mother Teresa," *New York Times*, August 15, 1982, http://www.nytimes.com/1982/08/15/world/hospital-is-visited-by-mother-teresa.html; Ann Rodgers, "Mother Teresa Revered for Putting Others First," *Pittsburgh Post-Gazette*, October 7, 2007, http://www.post-gazette.com/life/lifestyle/2007/10/07/Mother-Teresa-revered-for-putting-others-first/stories/200710070144; Ann Petrie and Jeanette Petrie, *Mother Teresa*, 1986, YouTube, http://www.youtube.com/watch?v=qnhiGtCBc10.

2   James Allan Francis, *One Solitary Life*, (n.p., n.d.), http://www.bartleby.com/73/916.html.

3   Ed Stetzer, "7 Principles to Lead as Jesus Led," ChristianityToday, September 27, 2017, http://www.christianitytoday.com/edstetzer/2017/september/7-principles-to-lead-as-jesus-led.html.

4   Pat Williams, *Coaching Your Kids to Be Leaders* (New York: Hachette, 2008), 113.

5   Robert Law, *The Emotions of Jesus* (New York: Charles Scribner's Sons, 1915), 100-101.

6   Max Lucado, *Life Lessons with Max Lucado: Book of James* (Nashville: Thomas Nelson, 2006), 36.

7   Martin Luther King. Jr., "Martin Luther King's Final Speech: 'I've Been to the Mountaintop'—The Full Text," (speech, Memphis, TN, April 3, 1968), ABCNews, http://abcnews.go.com/Politics/martin-luther-kings-final-speech-ive-mountaintop-full/story?id=18872817.

8   Dave Kraft, *Leaders Who Last* (Wheaton, IL: Crossway, 2010), 123.

9   Tom Peters, "Rules for Leaders (Continued)," *Fast Company*, February 28, 2001, https://www.fastcompany.com/42388/rules-leaders-continued.

10 See Matt. 8:14-17, Mark 1:29-31, Luke 4:38; see also 1 Cor. 9:5.

11 Alan Zimmerman, "A Bad Boss Is Bad For Business," DrZimmerman, https://www.drzimmerman.com/tuesdaytip/how-management-makes-or-breaks-a-companys-success.

12 Leaps: The Life Excelerator, "Dwight D. Eisenhower on Leadership," SELforSchools, https://selforschools.com/eisenhower.

13 Mark Bowden, "'Idiot,' 'Yahoo,' 'Original Gorilla': How Lincoln Was Dissed in His Day," *The Atlantic*, June 2013, https://www.theatlantic.com/magazine/archive/2013/06/abraham-lincoln-is-an-idiot/309304/.

14 Jane Arraf, Walter Rodgers, Alphonso Van Marsh, Barbara Starr, and Dana Bash, "'It Felt Good,' GI Says of Bush's Visit," CNN, November 28, 2003, http://www.cnn.com/2003/WORLD/meast/11/27/sprj.irq.main/.

15 Sam Walton, "10 Rules for Building a Business," Walmart, http://corporate.walmart.com/our-story/history/10-rules-for-building-a-business.

16 Billy Graham, *Just As I Am* (New York: HarperCollins, 1997), 127–128.

17 Ibid., 128–129.

18 Jia Tolentino, "Mike Pence's Marriage and the Beliefs That Keep Women from Power," *The New Yorker*, March 31, 2017, http://www.newyorker.com/culture/jia-tolentino/mike-pences-marriage-and-the-beliefs-that-keep-women-from-power.

19 Glennon Doyle Melton with Amanda Doyle, "Mike Pence's Marriage Rule Holds Women Back," *Time*, April 3, 2017, http://time.com/4723444/glennon-doyle-melton-pence-wife-jesus/.

20 Bob Herbert, "Sick and Abandoned," *New York Times*, September 15, 2005, http://www.nytimes.com/2005/09/15/opinion/sick-and-abandoned.html.

21 Leadership Vacuum Stymied Aid Offers," CNN, September 15, 2005, http://www.cnn.com/2005/US/09/15/katrina.response/.

22 Patrick Mortiere, "Timeline of Botched ObamaCare Rollout," *The Hill*, November 15, 2013, http://thehill.com/blogs/blog-briefing-room/news/190485-timeline-of-botched-implementation-of-obamacare; Tom Cohen, "Rough Obamacare Rollout: 4 Reasons Why," CNN, October 23, 2013, http://www.cnn.com/2013/10/22/politics/obamacare-website-four-reasons/index.html.

23 Daniel R Levinson, Inspector General, HHS, "HealthCare.gov: CMS Management of the Federal Marketplace—A Case Study," Health and Human Services, February 2016, https://oig.hhs.gov/oei/reports/oei-06-14-00350.pdf.

24 Johann Peter Lange, *A Commentary on the Holy Scriptures: Samuel* (New York: Charles Scribner's Sons, 1877), 456.

25 Stephen E. Ambrose, *Eisenhower: Soldier and President* (New York: Simon & Schuster, 1990), 16-17.

26 Ibid., 16.

27 Ibid., 44.

28 Matthew F. Holland, *Eisenhower Between the Wars: The Making of a General and Statesman* (Westport, CT: Greenwood, 2001), 188.

29 Eberhard Bethge, *Dietrich Bonhoeffer: A Biography* (n.p., n.d.), 927.

30 Charles Carleton Coffin, *Life of Lincoln* (New York: Harper & Brothers, 1892), 534.

31 Martin Luther King, Jr., "The Birth of a New Nation," (speech, Montgomery, Alabama, April 7, 1957), Social Justice Speeches, EdChange Multicultural Pavilion, http://www.edchange.org/multicultural/speeches/mlk_birth.html.

32 Pat Williams, *The Warrior Within: Becoming Complete in the Four Crucial Dimensions of Manhood* (Ventura, CA: Regal Books, 2006), 171.

33 Eddie Robinson and Richard Lapchick, *Never Before, Never Again: The Autobiography of Eddie Robinson* (New York: St. Martin's, 1999), 114.